20 RENTAL PROPERTIES IN ONE YEAR

by Graeme Fowler

First published September 2016

Cover Design and Layout: KA Design, Hastings

Printing: Graphicpress

ISBN 978-0-473-37229-3

Disclaimer

**This publication is designed to educate and provide general information regarding the subject matter covered. However, laws and practices often vary from time to time and are subject to change. Because each person's situation is different, specific advice should be tailored to the particular circumstances. For this reason, the reader is advised to consult with his or her own advisor regarding that individual's specific situation. The authors have taken reasonable precautions in the preparation of this book and believe the facts presented in the book are accurate as of the date it was written. However, neither the authors nor the publisher assume any responsibility for any errors or omissions. The authors and publisher specifically disclaim any liability resulting from the use or application of the information contained in this book, and the information is not intended to serve as legal advice related to individual situations.*

20 RENTAL PROPERTIES IN ONE YEAR

by Graeme Fowler

DEDICATION

This book is dedicated to all Property Investors, whether you're already retired or financially free, a full-time investor, or just starting out on your investment journey.

"It may be that when we no longer know which way to go that we have come to our real journey. The mind that is not baffled is not employed. The impeded stream is the one that sings".

"Always in the big woods, when you leave familiar ground and step off into a new place there will be, along with feelings of curiosity and excitement, a little nagging of dread. It is the ancient fear of the unknown, and it is your first bond with the wilderness you are going into. What you are doing is exploring. You are undertaking the first experience, not of the place, but of yourself in that place".

Both quotes by Wendell Berry

ACKNOWLEDGEMENTS

Firstly, I'd like to thank my wonderful partner Katrina for being so amazing. The last three years we've been together has been the best three years of my life, and one where I've found a new passion for real estate investing.

Also to my many mentors and teachers over the last 25 years – Robert Kiyosaki, John Burley, Blair Singer, DC Cordova, Brad Sugars, Tony Robbins, Roger Hamilton, Dave Rogers, Brendan Nichols, Mike Hancock, David Ure, Keith Cunningham, Esther Hicks (Abraham), Wayne Dyer, and Wayne Morgan.

To Richard & Amanda Lindsay and their daughter Charlotte for being such great friends over the last 15 years, and for all the fun times here and away on holidays together. Also Jeremy & Julz Haines, Jim Lowe, Andrew Dane, Tammy Onekawa for their friendship.

I thank my accountant Tony Weekes and his partner Pam Prior for their friendship and support over many years. Also thank you to Chris O'Connor & Joanne Cook at Strachan O'Connor for their friendship and legal support over many years.

In real estate sales, a big thankyou to David Scapens, Jason Whitaker, Paul Whitaker, Pam Prentor, Kaye Harrison, Kelly Riches, Richard & Ashleigh Liley, Tracey McCall, Fiona Marshall, Ronnie Turner, Nelson Raines and Lisa White.

To some of the trades-people and suppliers in real estate – Jarrod Macredie, Tom Leach, Jack Pritchard, Zane Alexander, Brett Person, Richard Alexander, Tammy Hessell, Kyle Clay, Steve Mills, Richard Jones, Toby Oosthuizen, Dan Jones, Steve Hewitt, Bart Mulder, Beau O'Brien, Sean Patrick, Kevin Fowler, and Craig Shearman.

Also to many of the really wonderful investors in Hawkes Bay that I helped mentor and coach in 2014/2015 – Mike & Steph Russell, Lacey Ward, Helen Gelletly, Tash Walker, Kim Potts, Brett Payne, Sarah King, Graeme Eagle, Dan Warren & Laura Harris, Sam Murdoch, Warren Murdoch, Gail Appleton, Stu McLean, Diana McKelvie, Karen & Gerry Molloy, Aaron Campion,

Dennis Lukies, Andrew Patullo, Kim Davey, Steffan & Kate Kelly, Tim Mapel, Keith Frankum, Michael Courtney, Nicola Fryer, Kim Davey, Julia & Jarrod Smith and many others.

In banking, thank you to Darrin McCormack, Judy Steiner, Mark Setford, Peter Norris, Andrea Snee, Bev Bibby, Mark Bibby and Lesley Smith.

A huge thank you also to my awesome property managers Katy Russell, Jamie Richardson, Tai Kekena, Barb Rangihuna, Chelsea Rangihuna, Alayna Strutt and Carole Paul.

And also to the many other friends and property investors over the last few years, especially Joelene Bagby, Lauren Worseley, Ankush Bajaj, UJ Rxy, Brett Harper, Leigh Fourie, Renee Kruger, Tiri Rangihuna, Caeli Gwynn, Scott Woods, Tom Alexander, Craig Chandler, Glenn Bride, Kitty Flisijn, Brian Neville, Maree Tassell, Lisa Dudson, Peter Ambrose, Shawn & Avonne Elliot, Brent & Anita Aitken-Taylor, Maggie Zabaglo, Amy and Bradley Ingram, Dean & Inka Jackson, Matt Harris, Nelly Smith, Bill & Chrissy Guthrie, Paul Ellis, Roger Hardie, Dave Smithson, Matt and Paul Wright, Dorien and Rineke Forster, Kaye Takarangi, Sunvi Ahsen, Angela Alexander and Fraser Toulmin, Emma Hagen, Laura Mursell, Michelle Berquist & Trent Jones, Steph Lawrence, Steve & Jill Norman, Kevin Heppleston, Kevin Tinker, Donna Ghaemaghamy, Ken Dentice, Tui Lewis, Rod Dalzell, Austin Mortimer, Jatinder Singh, Rick Behague, Ross Barnett, Naomi Hughes, Penny Darwin, Maddie Hamilton, Sue McDonald, Jo Harris, Richard Braddon-Parsons, Shane Storey, Donna Richardson, Henare & Nicole Harris, Donna Robinson, Beryl Le Grove, Pauline Beissel, Michelle Amy, Amy Parker, Brendon Johnson, Harry Skipper, Ruth Shannon, Samantha Rodgers, Nick Neilson, Amanda Elliot, Steve & Flo Pollard and Lynne Jackson.

And finally a big thanks to you for taking the time to read this book, to further your own development, your education, and your interest in property investing.

TABLE OF CONTENTS

PLEASE READ THIS FIRST

This book is put together so that you get maximum value from it, by starting to read it from the *introduction* and the *foreword*, right through to the end. While it may be tempting for some people to go straight to Part 3 where I talk about buying *20 Rental Properties In One Year*, you will not get anywhere near as much value from the book by doing that. You will only get a very small fraction of the potential value, and will most likely be left with more *questions* than answers.

The book is set out so that the information and the articles that you read, start building you a *foundation* of knowledge. And by the time you get to part three, you will be in a lot better place to understand, and receive it all. Even if you're an experienced investor or have read some of the articles previously, please read from the *start*, as you will get much more value from it.

Most of us like to take the *easy way out* in whatever it is that we're doing. It's easier to say 'no' to someone, it's easier to spend this $20 I have in my pocket than it is to save it, it's easier to walk away from a relationship because I don't like to talk about how I feel, it's easier to do nothing about my finances and hope that the government will take care of me when I'm 65. It's easier. The trouble with always taking the *easy way* out is that over a long period of time life will most likely, eventually become *very hard*. I decided at a young age to do the things that, *seemed* a lot harder at the time, being disciplined, regularly exercising, saving money etc, so that life would eventually become *easy*. And for the last 20+ years now, life has mostly been *very* easy, and lots of fun ☺

Every decision you make in life will take you further away, or closer to what it is that you want. Whether it's to do with your health, and not eating that piece of chocolate cake that you really know you shouldn't eat, or buying a new pair of shoes that you don't need because you feel bored; all these daily choices and decisions that you make, create who you are over a long period of time. People don't wake up one morning and suddenly become an Olympic athlete. Nor do they wake up one morning and suddenly become healthy, or suddenly have the knowledge and all it takes to become rich. It's our small daily decisions that build upon all our previous decisions over our life, that create who we are as a person. These small daily decisions all compound over time, and usually also determine how *happy* we are in life; and our own happiness and well-being is the most important thing of all.

Thank you for reading this, I hope you enjoy the book ☺

INTRODUCTION

"Even though there are days I wish I could change some things that happened in the past, there's a reason the rear view mirror is so small and the windshield is so big. Where you're headed is much more important than what you've left behind." Author unknown

Like my first book that was written in 2003, I struggled for a while to come up with anything to say for the introduction. This is how the intro in my first book started - and coincidentally today is also *July 28th* 2016.

It's now 6am on Monday, 28th July, 2003. Over the last week or so, I have been struggling as to what to put in the introduction. All the scripts have been done and ready for the final proofing before going to print, but still I had no idea what to write for this intro. As you will read later in my chapter, if you give your brain a task to do, something you don't know yet how to achieve, your subconscious will eventually work all out the answers for you—usually while you sleep.

This morning, I woke up—and knew exactly what needed to be in the introduction.

A *lot* has changed since 2003, and things have also changed since the *update* and revised edition of that book which was done in 2008.

Everything is in a constant state of change. For a lot of people, things do keep changing over and over, but they keep changing to the *same* thing. This has the illusion that things are always staying the same, when they are in fact – constantly changing. Even our own bodies are in a constant state of change and most cells in our body are not the cells we had seven years ago. Some cells regenerate more slowly like our bones which take 7 – 10 years to completely replace the cells, our liver cells regenerate within a few months and some cells regenerate within only a few days, such as our stomach lining and our skin.

LAW OF ATTRACTION

Why does it appear then that some people just can't get ahead in life, things *aren't* changing for them for the better? As I mentioned, they are changing, but they're changing to what looks like is the *same* thing, over and over again. Why does this happen? It happens because their attention is on 'what is' and not what they want. It's more focused on what they *don't* like or *don't* want, and *that* brings them more of the same. In other words what people are focused on or what they give their *attention* to, is what they will attract more of. For someone that has very little money to spare each week, or going more and more into debt, their focus is on 'what is' and not what they really want. It's like a stick with two ends, in this case *wanted* and *unwanted*. Where someone's attention and thoughts mostly are about any particular situation, will show up as a *result* of where they are *now*. Every choice and decision you have made in your life adds up and results in where you are right now. If you don't like where you are right now, whether it's the lack of money, poor health or an unhappy relationship, the first step is to understand that *you* created it. Take responsibility for where you are and don't blame anyone else for where you may be right now, and that includes your parents. Thank your parents for everything that *works* in your life, and take *responsibility* for everything that doesn't. That's more empowering than blaming other people for what's not working in your life. If you blame others for where you are now, it appears to let you off the hook, but avoids responsibility and costs you *your* happiness.

We all create our own *reality* whether we like to admit it or not. We are where we are now as a result of *all* the choices we've made in life. We are continually in the act of creation, it occurs uninterrupted. That is, it *never stops*. Every thought, every word, and every deed is creative. Every vibration released from every cell in your body *recreates* you, and your entire reality, anew. You are being changed in every single moment. Your future is produced in tiny increments, not in one fell swoop or with any one big decision. It's the *increments* to which you must pay attention. Then the *more* major moments and the *big* decisions in your life will take care of themselves. Your health, wealth, relationships and *overall* happiness are all created moment by moment. They are created by the choices only *you* can make every day. These daily choices all add up, accumulate, and result in how healthy you are, how wealthy you are, how the relationships are with the people around you are, and how *happy* you are. You get to choose in all of these areas, every day.

So, how do we change a situation that we're in that we don't like? Firstly, by understanding and knowing that it was *us* that created it to begin with. Secondly, by accepting 'what is' or *'what's so'* as being okay, and not making it wrong in any way.

N.B. Making where you are 'wrong' only attracts more of the same to you, as that's where your focus is. Shouting 'no' at something doesn't make it go away, it only brings more of it to you, as that's where your attention is. The universe does not understand 'no', it only understands 'yes'. If you shout 'no' at something that you do not want or do not like, it's the same as saying 'bring to me this thing that I do not want'. We live in an attraction based universe and so where your attention is focused, is what you will attract more of. If you look at anything unwanted and the attention other people give to it, it simply creates more of the unwanted.

Have you ever had an argument or falling out with someone and want to avoid seeing them or talking to them at all costs? And then you keep bumping into them up town or in the supermarket. Saying or thinking 'no' to wanting them near you, is what brings them closer to you!

Another example is, look at the war on terrorism, the war on cancer, the war on drugs, the war on poverty, the war against anything, the problems keep getting bigger. Mother Teresa once said "I was once asked why I don't participate in anti-war demonstrations. I said that I will never do that, but as soon as you have a pro-peace rally, I'll be there".

It's not that we all should be in denial about everything going on, but by paying attention to something and shouting 'no' at it, you are actually making the problem worse, not better. Most people mean well, their intentions are good. But they also don't realise that observing things they don't like and talking about how bad it is to others, rather than making things better, is actually spreading the problem and making it worse.

Here's an over simplified solution which you can use in most cases. If you see anything you don't like or you don't agree with, then it is none of your business. But if you see something you do like, then it is your business.

After understanding that we all created our own lives up until this point, and nobody else is to blame for where we are now, *and* you can accept fully

100% that it's all okay, only *then* you can do something about it. We must make peace with where we are *before* we can create what it is that we *do* want.

So now how can we do that? I've seen and read about many different ways to create what it is that we really do want, and one of the main ones I've used a lot in the past was affirmations. I wrote about this in some detail in my first book; however I now think affirmations do have their limitations. They don't seem to work for a lot of people, unless they can use the affirmations day in and day out for what may be many years, and most people will give up well before this. Also if they continue to *doubt* that they will achieve the goal or what it is they want, affirmations can become very frustrating after a while.

This method here below is the best one I've seen and like for creating, or manifesting, anything that you are wanting. It applies also if you are using it for goal setting.

1. **Vision**: have an idea, image, dream, wish, picture of what you say you want. Have some initial concept or vision.
2. **Desire**: this goes hand in hand with the idea of excitement. The things that you see that you say you want must be accompanied by a strong energy and strong emotion. Emotion equals energy in motion.
3. **Belief**: you must know, explore, examine within yourself that you have the belief that it is *possible* to manifest this thing and that you *deserve* it. Your beliefs are going to allow this thing to be possible.
4. **Acceptance**: you must totally accept yourself and the new belief as true, without question, without a shadow of a doubt. Just as you accepted the old belief.
   N.B. All a belief is, is this; it's a thought you keep thinking over and over and over again. You've thought it hundreds and maybe even thousands of times before it until it finally <u>creates</u> a belief. After you create this belief, you will keep finding new evidence to support this belief, and discard or filter out everything that disagrees with it. We all have so many beliefs that we don't even think <u>are</u> beliefs. We believe them all to be <u>the</u> truth. Beliefs such as 'life is hard, or life is a struggle', 'you have to work hard for your money', 'men always leave me in relationships', 'women only want to control me', 'when things are going so well - you know something bad is going to happen soon',

'there's a god up in the sky looking at everything we do and judging us, making up his mind up if we're going to heaven or hell', 'I've always been a shy person ever since I was a baby' or 'eating certain types of food will cause cancer' just to name a few beliefs.

5. **Intention:** You must *intend* to manifest it. You can want something, but not necessarily intend it. It must be a conscious *choice*. Not an effort, but a focus.
6. **Action:** you must act like you're *already* in the state of that reality that you want. You must *behave* as if the reality *already exists* in the present. You must do the things you would do, in the way you would do them – as if the reality already existed for you.
7. **Detach/Allowance:** lastly you must absolutely, totally detach from *any* outcome at all. You have to <u>*let it go*</u>. Utterly and *unconditionally* let it go. That's the power of paradox. You have to have, in order to manifest anything, an absolute intensity of what you want - with absolutely *no expectation* that it has to manifest at all. You have to let it go totally. And also know that everything is already perfect as it is. Once you accept that the way it is now, is perfect, then the way it is, can become another way. It will manifest in the best possible way if you build up that intensity of intention - and then just let it go. No expectations, no structure, no insistence. Just total allowance.

It's a bit like using a GPS when going from one destination to another. If you're driving from say Tauranga to Wellington following the GPS's route set out for you, you have to trust that you will arrive in Wellington at some point in time. You could be driving along and thinking "I don't see any sign of Wellington yet and I've been driving for hours, maybe I should *turn back* now. This is so stupid. I don't ever think I'm ever going to get to Wellington, I can see a long way in front of me, but I *still* can't see even a glimpse of it. I must be doing this all wrong, the GPS is wrong, it's giving me wrong directions. I will play it safe and go back to Tauranga, a place I know well and is comfortable for me". You won't see any sign of Wellington until 99.99% of your journey is complete. It can be the same with manifesting, and also goal setting for something specific that you want. You may not have any *physical* evidence of what you want *until* it actually happens.

Further on in this book there are quite a few articles I've written and one of those is titled 'The Pitfalls and *Stress* of Goal Setting/Planning'. After reading that article, come back and read this part again as it may make more sense to you then, if it doesn't already at this point. In summary to all of this and to simplify it a little; you want to be as happy *now* and feel as good *now* in the present, as you *would* feel as if you had *already* reached/achieved the goal, or had created the thing that you wanted to create. For example, let's say you are not currently in a relationship but want to be. By focusing on the fact that you are lonely, or not having a partner *isn't* the answer to finding a new one. You need to find the feeling and the happiness *as if* you already had the partner. Or if you want more money or better cash-flow, you need to be as happy now and feel the same way, as if you had the money or the cash-flow right now. To be as happy *now* and feel as good *now* as if it were *already* true.

It may be difficult to understand *why* this works if this is all quite new to you; I just know that it does work.

This is a quote that I really love, often think about, and have come to know and understand more and more every day – 'The Universe is full of magical things, patiently waiting for our wits to grow sharper'.

So, what has changed for me since writing the updated book "NZ Real Estate Investors' Secrets" in 2008?

UPDATE SINCE 2008

That was eight years ago now and a lot *has* changed, and also a lot has changed to the *same* thing ☺

I was still recovering financially from losing about $1.5 million in 2005/2006, which I wrote about in detail in my updated book in 2008.

N.B. That book has now sold almost 15,000 copies with only about 200 copies currently left which I have at home. These will all be sold I would imagine in the next six months or so, as people still ask for them occasionally. The distributor that was selling them throughout NZ went into liquidation in 2010 so I ended up with a few thousand books at home. If you would like a copy, you can e-mail me at orion8@xtra.co.nz *and I will let you know if I still have any available. If not, I can e-mail you a pdf file of the book for $15, as it's not available on Kindle.*

Also the property market in Hawkes Bay here had peaked around 2006/2007 and prices were slowly going down. This happened gradually from about 2007 to 2013 when prices steadied again. From 2006 to 2013, the market prices of the properties I owned dropped in value by between 25% and

30%. I didn't do a lot of buying in that time, it was more of a time of consolidation and making sure the foundation of the portfolio was sound.

Then in 2010 I separated from my long term partner of 16 years. With the settlement from that I had to sell off more properties. I had gone from owning 65 properties in 2005, down to only 37 properties by 2012. Fortunately I had followed my own advice and continued to pay down debt slowly over this time, so even though property values were dropping, my overall LVR (loan to value ratio) didn't change that much and was still around 50% LVR in 2012.

In 2012 I also sold my Mr Rental franchise in Hawkes Bay. I had started it in September 2002 and when it came time to renew the 10 year franchise, a lot of the rules had changed. I initially bought the franchise as it was a great cash-flow business that had excellent systems in place. This meant if it was set up well and you had great employees, the owner didn't have to be in the business 40 hours a week like with so many other businesses or franchises. A lot of the buyers of the franchises in 2002 – 2003 were in a similar position to me, wanting a business that could be set up and run effectively by the employees, with very little input from the franchisee.

One of the many rules that had changed over the years was that the franchisor now wanted all the franchisees to work in the office for a minimum of 25 – 30 hours a week. My time in the office had up until that time, averaged about two or three hours a week over the entire 10 years that I owned the business. Even though it required very little input from me, it was still one of, if not *the* most profitable out of all the 20 or so Mr Rental franchises in NZ. This didn't matter to the franchisors and they wanted me to be in the office for at least 25 hours every week, apart from having a few weeks off each year for a holiday. Even though the cash-flow from the business was great and it had been earning me around $20,000 a month profit for quite a number of years up until that point, it was a very easy decision for me to sell it. My time was worth more to me than having a passive income of $5,000 or so a week, but having to sit in an office for 25 – 30 hours every week, to keep getting it. The business was therefore sold and all settled in late August 2012 to the new owners who still own it today. Luckily, in early 2008 I had bought a commercial building for the business to go in, which I purchased privately for $500,000. I took out an 8yr P & I loan which was paid back in full in early 2016. The new owners now lease the building from me and there's no debt on the building. When you own a business that needs premises like this, it makes a lot more sense to buy a building, and have *your business* as the tenant. Even if the loan was for 10 – 15 years, it's far better to *buy* than it is to lease off someone else. There's often not a lot of difference in *cost* between buying and leasing, but with buying, you're gaining *equity* every month, and slowly paying off the mortgage until you *own* it outright.

From 2008 up until 2012 I had done very little in property investing and was kind of in cruise mode, not needing to do a lot at all. After selling the business in 2012, I started focusing more on property and started looking at properties again, buying the odd property here and there to reno/trade. A lot of my time and focus was also spent on finding another partner after Tracey and I had separated in 2010. I went on many dates and had several short term relationships, as well as one of around 14 months. None of these were what I was really looking for and I was kind of drifting along with the property investing during this time as well. I was still doing my walk up Te Mata Peak seven days a week and was overall still very happy.

Meeting My New Partner Katrina

It was early in 2012 when I met Katrina. She was happily married with three kids and we met through my son Ryan and one of her sons being in the same class at school. Ryan was seven years old at the time and had been go-karting already for a couple of years by that time. We had recently bought a newer go-kart and were wanting to sell his old one. Ryan had talked a lot about his karting in his class at school and how he had won the club championship in his 'cadet' class for ages six up to age eleven. He had won it in his first year racing at only six years of age, competing against boys who were a lot older than him. His good friend Corbyn was keen to find out how he could also get into the sport. Corbyn and his dad Dennis came out to the track and watched Ryan and the other boys all race at one of the monthly club days, and were now very keen to buy a go-kart as well. I mentioned we were selling his other go-kart and so they came around home to have a look. Katrina had asked Dennis before this, what I did for a job to be able to afford the go-karting sport, which can be very expensive. He mentioned that he thought I didn't have a job, and so now both were quite curious how I could afford it. Dennis asked me what I did so I told him I was a property investor, and gave him a copy of my book to read.

The next day he called me and asked if I could come out to the orchard where they lived to chat about their own property. Katrina and her husband Dennis lived on the orchard just out of Havelock North and owned the 10 acre block with her parents. The orchard was leased with three residential properties on it. Katrina's parents now wanted to sell their ½ share in the property and move back to Levin, and so now the property was on the market to sell. Neither of them really wanted to sell but thought there was no way of being able to buy her parents out and still keep the orchard. They had now just received an offer on the property, and Katrina's parents wanted her and Dennis to sign it so they could sell and move on. I went through some figures with them and showed how it might be possible for them to buy her parents out and still keep the property. If they rented out the house where her parents were living next to them, plus the income from the other property on the site, as well as the orchard lease, it seemed possible. I told them to wait before agreeing to anything or signing the offer, and I would put them in touch with a very good mortgage broker in Napier, Judy Steiner.

Katrina met with Judy the next day and went through all their financials to see if it was at all possible to buy her parents' share of the property. Judy said yes it all looked possible that it could get approved, subject to it valuing up to a certain figure. I put her in contact with a valuer I had used many times before, so he could come out and value the property. They signed a contract with her parents to buy them out, subject to the finance being approved. Within a few days the loan was approved, and they were now able to buy the other ½ share of the orchard. The only issue was it was a huge amount of debt, and Katrina being the one that mostly looked after their finances was quite concerned about it. I said it would be okay, the only risk would be if interest rates went up a few percent, cash-flow may get a little tight to pay the mortgage. They agreed to the finance offer and went unconditional on the contract with her parents. A couple of times Katrina asked me if she could come and talk to me about taking on so much more debt and how worried she was about it, as she had nobody else she could talk to about it. I reassured her again that it wasn't really a lot of money and the incomes from the property would cover it all fine.

Once it all went through she was more comfortable about it and they invited me around home for a roast dinner to say thanks for helping them with it all. Katrina had also been interested in property investing for many years prior to this having read quite a few books about it, but had never been in a position to be able to invest. She had enjoyed reading my book and started asking me some questions about property investment, and owning rentals.

A month or so later on Anzac Day 2012, Katrina asked if she could do the Te Mata Peak walk with me and ask a few more questions about property investing. I said yes that's fine as long as you can walk and ask questions at the same time. All was fine for the first 20 minutes walking mostly downhill, until we started to go up the goat track, which is very tough going if you aren't fit or used to it. After getting about half way up the goat track, Katrina said for me to go on and wait for her at the top. I said okay, Kobi (my dog) will walk with you and I will see you at the top. I got to the top and there was no sign of Katrina. After 10 minutes or so I asked a couple of other walkers who had walked up if they had seen a woman and a dog on the track. They said yes they had seen her and she was resting a bit further down. Another five minutes later and I saw Kobi walking up, he had given up waiting and now come up to see me! I called her mobile and she said she was going to go back down, as it was too tough going up the hill. She had made it to only five minutes or so from the top and I said it was crazy to go back down as it would take so much longer. So she started walking again and eventually made it to the top and saying she would never do that again. However, the next day she wanted to walk again and ask me some more questions. This time we did an easier walk, and as time went by she did the goat track again and walked with me a couple of times each week, always asking me lots of questions. She also talked to me about the women I was going on dates with at the time and many of them were very funny stories.

About six months later we had become good friends and she had also lost a lot of weight and was now able to keep up with me walking! We both entered into the Peak Trail Blazer in November 2012 which is a 12.8kms walking *or* running race. I came 3rd in the men's walking race and Katrina came 1st in the women's race which was a huge achievement, given that it was even steeper than the goat track we were used to doing.

As time went by we kept in contact and I was still going on lots of dates, about 25 - 30 I think just in the time we had been walking together for seven months. It wasn't until several months later in early 2013 that there was even a mention, or a thought that I was interested in her, or her in me. She was happily married and I hadn't even considered Katrina as being someone I would have ever even dated, let alone been in a relationship with. However something changed one day and I don't even know what triggered it, it was all very weird how one day it was just so different. We talked about it and then in February 2013 Katrina told her husband what had happened. He was naturally very upset and it was not a nice time for any of us.

A month later in March 2013 Katrina ended up moving in with me and has been with me ever since. We bought a house together less than two years later and have an extremely solid relationship/partnership and are the very best of friends. It has all worked out well, Dennis and Katrina are still very good friends and he comes around most days to see his kids and often has dinner with us, and also does the walk up Te Mata Peak with us occasionally. He started walking Te Mata Peak after they separated and soon became very fit. We competed as a three-person team in The Cape Kidnappers 32km walking race in November 2013, and the 50km Triple Peaks walking race in 2014, winning both of these events.

Over the 3 ½ years we've been together now, Katrina and I have done many local and overseas trips together and have also done five cruises. Four of these cruises have been with her parents coming with us, and three of the cruises were also with her three kids coming along, and my son Ryan.

A far as property and finances go, Katrina is very ambitious and wants to be able to support herself financially independent of me. This is one thing I really love about her and enjoy supporting her to work towards achieving this. You will read later on about how I bought 20 properties with 'no equity' used in 2014, which is the main focus of this book. Dennis and Katrina set up a similar situation where they now own six rental properties together in a new property trust that was set up in 2014. They also still own the orchard together, with the three properties on it.

The other big step towards Katrina's becoming *financially independent* happened recently. She was working at a 9am – 2pm job as the payroll manager for the DHB five days a week up until last month, June 2016. I had asked her what her 'overall happiness' scale was on a scale of 1 – 10 a few months before this and she said it was a '7'. I was quite surprised and thought it would have been higher than that and asked why it was only a '7'. She said she really didn't like her job and working for a government organisation, and the way they did things.

A few weeks later, I had the idea that I could employ her on a contract type arrangement and she would get the same income as she was currently getting from her job. Katrina could help me a little with what I was doing with any renovation projects, but the main focus would be for her to do some renos/

trades for herself. The profit she made would go towards paying back the money I would be paying her each year. I would also be guarantor on the loans for the properties she was buying, and also pay the 20% deposit needed to settle each property, as well as the renovation costs. She liked the idea but was very unsure about giving up the security of the job she had been in for about nine years.

After thinking about it for a week or so, Katrina said yes and handed in her notice at work giving them nearly two months notice. She also set up a new company to do the trades in, as GST would have to be claimed upon purchasing and paid back upon selling the properties.

So far in less than two months, Katrina has already purchased four properties to reno and sell on again in the trading company she set up. The first property was bought, renovated and sold within six weeks or so, only just settling a week ago. The profit on this one was approx $46,000 incl GST after all expenses, holding costs etc. This gives her an after tax profit of about $28,000. The 2nd property that was purchased has been renovated and is currently under contract and had three offers on it. The profit on this one will be a lot less, but still a reasonable amount at around $20,000 after all expenses. The 3rd one hasn't settled yet and is due to settle in the next two weeks. With this one, we have prior access to renovate the property and hope to have it all ready to market by the time it settles. She is aiming for a profit of around $20,000 on this one as well. The 4th one is another renovation project which settles in September and will hopefully give her a profit of a little over $25,000. The profits may seem quite small on the last three compared to the first reno, but I think it's more important to do a lot of smaller profit deals, than wait and try to get one with a big profit in it. This way it also gives her a lot more experience. Experience in what to look for when buying, what needs doing and what doesn't need doing, how much to spend, what adds value and what doesn't add value, and just the overall process of buying, renovating and selling property. What she's already put into place so far should earn her well over $100,000 (before tax) in the two months since leaving her job. So since leaving work at the beginning of last month, I think it's a great start for her, and Katrina is also very pleased with the results. The next step will be for her to use the income from trading and renovating properties to purchase some more long term buy and hold rentals, and have them all paid off within a maximum of 20 years.

Property Seminars

Going back now to 2014, while I was buying the 20 properties that you will later read about in this book, I also started to run some free property investment seminars in Hawkes Bay, just for local investors. I initially did a two-hour beginners seminar for a group of 40 local investors that I know, and then another seminar for 40 investors who were clients of Property Brokers Hastings/Napier. The condition was that Property Brokers would allow me to use their office in Havelock North for free to run an investment seminar for people that I knew, on the condition that I would do another seminar for a group of 40 property investors they had on their database. I also mentioned after each seminar that I was available for the next 12 months for free if anyone wanted to catch up with me for a coffee or lunch. This would be to go over their own personal plan/strategy and the goals they wanted to achieve. Some were already experienced investors owning more than 15 properties, and some were just starting out. Each week I met up with these people for a coffee or over lunch, usually having at least five or six appointments a week.

I also ran another seminar a few weeks later which was a more advanced one, and combined the two groups of 40 people and around 60 investors attended that one. From there I ran another one just on negotiations, and then another one a month later on goal setting and planning. Over the 12 months I did many more free seminars, one was on property management with my property managers being there, one on tax with an accountant, another one was with a good friend of mine Maree Tassell who runs a property finding business based in Rotorua, one on renovations and trading, and one with a question and answer session with myself, as well as some other local property experts. All up from memory there were 10 or 11 seminars I did for free over the 12 months. I also met up with almost all of the investors individually, some of them at least seven or eight times during the year.

One of these couples was Mike and Steph Russell in Hastings. Mike at the time was President of the HB Property Investors' association, and has kindly written the 'Foreword' for this book.

This coaching/mentoring was all very rewarding for me and I enjoyed the interaction with the people and helping them with their plan and their goals. Many times I would go with them to look at properties they were looking at buying. I think almost all of the investors bought at least one property over the next 12 – 18 months, and some bought at least five properties.

Facebook Investor Group

After the first two seminars, I also set up a Facebook Group for all these investors to ask any questions in, or post any property deals they had bought or were looking at buying. I posted the deals I was buying as well, whether they were buy and holds in the new trust I set up in 2014, or any renovation/trades I was doing. With the renovation projects, I put up before and after photos, as well as the purchase price, total reno costs and then the overall profit made on each deal. Photos of the buy and holds were also posted to the group, along with the purchase prices, yields etc.

Earlier this year, I opened the Facebook group up to other property investors around NZ to be a part of as well. I also changed the name to "Property Investors Chat Group NZ". It has now grown from the original 60 members we had in 2014, to well over 1,500 members only five months later in July 2016.

If *you* would also like to join this property investor group on Facebook, you can search for it in the 'groups' section on Facebook, or send me a personal message on Facebook so I can copy and paste this link to you:- https://www.facebook.com/groups/340682962758216/?hc_location=ufi&__mref=message

Alternatively, you can e-mail me on orion8@xtra.co.nz and request the link to join.

People often ask me about mentoring them, and at this stage I'm still not doing any ongoing mentoring/coaching. The only thing I am doing occasionally is a one hour sit down chat with people about where they currently are, and what they want to achieve. This is the same as what I was doing for the HB investors in 2014/2015, although that was all done for free. For this type of consultation which is not advice, only my opinion on what I would do in a similar situation, it is $400 + GST for one hour. This is generally for investors that already own five properties or more and want some direction, or redirection, to help them achieve what they want from their investing.

New LVR Rules 2016

So, as you can see, there have been a lot of changes in the last eight years or so since doing the update for my last book. One thing that has only just changed in the last week or so with *property investing* in New Zealand is the new LVR rules. Up until last week, most banks or lenders would lend investors 80% of the purchase price *or* of a valuation, whichever was the *lower*. Now with this most recent change in rules with the Reserve Bank of NZ getting involved in trying to slow the property market down, investors will now need a *40%* deposit to purchase a property, as opposed to only needing a 20% deposit. Also for any trades or renovation projects, you will also need a 40% deposit. This rule was supposed to have started as of September 1st 2016, but has already been put in place by the banks, unless you have a pre-approval. The 3rd renovation/trade property I mentioned earlier that Katrina is buying has already been affected by this. This one was purchased privately and the bank couldn't find any comparable sales nearby for the desktop valuation (E-Value) and so has used the GV (RV, CV) to base their lending on. The GV is significantly lower than her purchase price. And with the bank only lending 60% of this amount, it means the deposit needed for this one is going to be well over 50% of the purchase price! I haven't had a situation previously where a bank couldn't find any comparable sales to one I was purchasing, so it is very unusual. Going forward the next properties purchased will hopefully require only a 40% deposit.

This all goes to show that the banks can change their rules at any time. The government can also change the law, the rules, their regulations and requirements, at any time. This is something I've mentioned on a few occasions in some of the articles I've written over the last 14 years, and are also here in this book for you to read.

There isn't anything you or I can do about all this, it's just the way it is and we have to accept it. It's the same with any rule, regulation, policy, law etc – we may not agree with it, but we must work within these rules the best we can. Another thing is this. Most of the time new rules and regulations like this that come in, the very people they say they *want* to help are the ones that will be the *worst* off. If a certain amount of investors are no longer able to buy rental properties, there are fewer properties available to rent, and therefore fewer properties to choose from. It comes down to supply and demand, and if there aren't enough rental houses available to rent, it will push rents up even more. Then people wanting to buy their first home (those the government wants to help) will be paying more rent, and are able to save even less each week for a deposit on their first home.

So, nobody knows how long the 40% deposit will stay as it is for investors, however I don't think it will stay like it is for too long. Especially if it takes a lot of investors out of the market as I mentioned, and prevents them from buying rental properties. 40% is a lot of amount of money to come up with, even in Hawkes Bay where prices are fairly low compared to other places around NZ. For example, if someone wants to purchase a rental property for $260,000 – the deposit on this would be $104,000.

Already in the last week or so of this new rule coming into place, I've heard of eight deals not going through now because of this new rule. Plus other investors that *were* in a position to buy are no longer in that position, and are unable to make successful offers, because they don't have enough money now for the deposit. If it does take a big chunk of investors out of the market like I think it will, it won't take too long before there aren't enough rental properties to go around for all those people who need to rent.

More Households Renting

In 1991, a year or so after I started investing in property, 26% of households rented, and by 2001 this had grown to 30%. Now in 2016 home ownership is at an even lower level with approximately 35% of houses being rented.

This trend still seems to be going up slowly and I think that has to do with a couple of things.

Firstly it's easier for people to buy all the things that depreciate so quickly such as cars, big screen TVs, appliances, computers etc on *no* or very low deposit, or they can simply put it on a credit-card or a store-card. It creates a situation where people want something *now*, they have to have it today, but they don't go through the process or the discipline of saving the money for a deposit. They can just pay it off over time. Less and less people are able to save *any* money each week; they simply spend it all and have nothing left.

Payday loans are a big thing in the U.S. If someone runs out of money before they run out of *month*, they can get a payday loan which gives them the cash *now* to get them through until their next payday. Generally people in the U.S. get paid monthly and it's very common for people to run out of money before the start of the next month when they get paid again. Payday loans give them the ability to borrow money today, usually up to $500 and then pay it back to the lender when they get paid next. The amount of interest they get charged to do this is usually between $10 and $30 *per* week for *every* $100 they borrow. So if someone borrowed $400 to get them through until their next payday in two weeks time, they would pay anywhere from $80 up to $240 in *interest* for the privilege of having the money *now*. NZ also has payday loans now, although at this stage we don't hear too much about them. Maybe they will become a bigger part of people's lives here too in the future, but hopefully not.

Apart from buying a house, people can have almost all the things they wish to buy. Buy it today and pay it off over time. They don't think of the overall or the total cost, only 'how much is it a week?' The trouble with doing this is that they pay a huge amount of interest, which makes it even more difficult to get ahead financially.

Tax Freedom Day

The second reason I believe that people find it harder to get ahead financially today, and therefore more difficult to save for a deposit on a house, is *tax*. Why tax? There's something that not a lot of people know about called our 'Tax Freedom Day'. This is a theoretical day during the year that if you look at your total income and the total amount of tax you pay each year, this is the first day of the year in which your money would be all yours. In other words, let's say for example you pay a total of 20% in tax on your earnings during the year; the other 80% is yours to keep. 20% of the year equates to 73 days, and day 73 of this year was March 13th. So March 13th in this example would be your 'Tax Freedom Day'. The other 80% of the year being 293 days, all that money from then on is yours to keep. In the early 1900's tax was very low and 'Tax Freedom Day' was around January 22nd in the United States. I don't know what it was in New Zealand, but I imagine it would be much the same. Over the years, governments have added more and more taxes into our lives which we all must pay, and this theoretical 'Tax Freedom Day' keeps getting pushed further and further out during the year. In NZ this year, our 'Tax Freedom Day' was May 21st. This means that all the money you earn this year; up until the 21st May, all of it goes to the government in various forms of tax. From May 22nd until the end of the year, that is all yours to keep. Another way of looking at it is, let's say you pay all your tax at the start of the year and when you have finished paying it, you can keep the rest. You would have to work from the start of the year January 1st up until May 21st for the government, and not keep anything. After May 21st you're allowed to keep the rest of the money you earn until the end of that year.

Some countries are even worse than us in NZ and have to work up until the end of *July* for their 'Tax Freedom Day', meaning that less than half the money they earn is theirs to keep; over half of it goes in taxes.

You may have heard of something called 'The Boston Tea Party'. This happened in the late 1700's and if you're interested you can read a lot more about it if you search for it on Google. In brief, it was an uproar from the masses to a tax imposed on 'tea', and involved the U.S. and the British Empire. How much was the tax they were imposing? Only a 3% tax! We pay 15% GST on everything we buy and don't even give it a thought. Now hundreds of years later, governments add more and more taxes to our lives and hardly anyone ever questions it. The new taxes they introduce seem to get more and more ridiculous as time goes on. Now many governments are looking at or have already introduced a 'sugar' tax on soft drinks etc. We already have around 100 various taxes in various disguises in our lives now. Some of the more well known ones being income tax, company tax, trust income tax, goods and services tax, property taxes (rates), a tax for selling a property within two years, registration fees for dogs, environmental taxes, alcohol tax, road tax (on diesel vehicles), petrol taxes, tobacco tax etc just to name a few. Then there are all the other hidden costs or indirect taxes disguised in one form or another. Such things as a 'licence' to get married, a driver licence (which used to be free), passports, building application fees, council permits to install a woodburner, council contribution costs to sub-divide a property, parking fines, speeding fines, registration costs, ACC costs and many more. I heard many years ago that it costs the U.S. government at least 61c to raise $1 in tax. How accurate that is I don't know, but just think about how many politicians there are and the income they make plus all their perks. Also think of how many different government organisations there are, how many employees that work for the government throughout NZ including the IRD, WINZ, CYFS and all the hundreds of buildings they lease etc. Who is actually paying for all this? Then there are all the people on some kind of welfare, the unemployment benefit, the sickness benefit, the DPB, and everyone over the age of 65 also receives a pension until they die.

Tax the Rich More?

Is it any wonder why people who don't understand the bigger picture, want to tax the rich even *more* and give it to all the people that don't have money? The people who own businesses and are paying huge taxes like myself, people who are already paying hundreds of thousands of dollars a year in tax already, are the ones they want to tax even more. Unfortunately there is no easy answer because governments have *created* this type of society over many, many years where people expect handouts for doing nothing. People aren't able to support themselves financially and so have been taught to rely on *others* for their money. It's not their fault. It's the result of government policies that have been put in place over time, that have created it all. There are exceptions to this, and we will always have some people who really do need help and are unable to support themselves financially. They will always need this help, but I'm talking about the overall way it has been *created* slowly over many years.

For example up until the 1970's there was no domestic purposes benefit in NZ. Families or the partners of women having children always managed to support them. Once the DPB came into being, a few women looked at this as an *easier* option. The government could help them, and so they didn't have to rely on an ex partner or their own family for money. Over the years, more and more women chose this as an easier option and many even making it a way of life, not giving it a second thought. Now there are over 110,000 women on the DPB and this costs tax payers about $40 million a week, or $2 billion a year. It also seems that there's no limit to the amount of kids someone can have, which is all well and good *if* they can support themselves and their family, but *not* if they expect everyone else to pay for them. Especially if they complain that they don't get enough money to support their family, and say that it's because all the rich people aren't being taxed enough. In some ways you can't blame them for this however, as I say it was the government who introduced this and created the *demand* for it. It would be like offering every worker in NZ say $80,000 per annum for doing *nothing*, or the *choice* to work and still receive the same money. How many people would work? Very few I would suggest.

So it's little wonder that things are the way they are now. My Dad grew up in a very large family, he was the youngest of eight kids, but his parents didn't ask anyone else for money if they didn't have enough to get by. One parent could work and have enough money to support their spouse and their children. Now many years later, most families need both parents working just to get by, and the kids will often have to go into an after-school programme until their parents finish work at 5pm or later. People are working harder and harder and also longer hours, some taking on more than one job just to keep up. If you also think of the unemployment benefit, a temporary help for the people who are out of work. We now have some families over several generations who have *never* worked in their life, and have always relied on the unemployment benefit for their income each week. However, many politicians and the people with not a lot of money will blame the rich people for their situation and financial problems saying things like 'the wealth gap keeps getting bigger and bigger, the rich are getting richer and the poor are getting poorer'! This may be true, but not for the reason they think it is. They believe that wealthy people are taking a piece of *their* pie, when in reality the wealthy are just making a *bigger* pie for everyone to share.

If you think back to 50 years ago and all the money that was in circulation in one form or another then in NZ, and compare to how much money there is in circulation now. The population is a lot larger, and so is the total pool of money, or the economy. If there was a certain (total) amount of money around 50 years ago, and now it has grown exponentially to hundreds of times more than it was back then, how did that happen? You may say there are more people today, or inflation etc, but *how* did that create more money? A new baby being born doesn't *add* money into our economy, nor does inflation. What does create more money is an expanding of the *overall* pie of money; this is through the wealthy making it a bigger pie for all through production, business etc, and it just appears that the poorer and less fortunate people get less of it.

The wealthy usually do get wealthier and the poor often stay where they are with very little, so of course the gap is going to get bigger. If the politicians could somehow make it a new law that everyone was now equal and we all had exactly say $100,000 in cash/equity, within 10 years there would be a similar gap again in wealth as there is now. It would revert back to the rich getting richer and the poor getting poorer. Even within one year you would find some people with no money once again, and others would already be multi-millionaires. The wealth would very quickly revert back to how things are again now. How would that happen? Part of it is peoples' mindset, part of it is peoples' spending, or money habits, part of it is to do with planning and goal setting, part of it is education, part of it is financial intelligence, and part of it is 'deservability' (how much you believe you deserve in life).

SUMMARY

In summary of what has turned out to be a much longer introduction than I had originally intended, a lot has changed for me in the last few years. And a lot of what has changed for the better has been a *result* of some of the things that have changed to the *same* thing; such things as my mindset, my overall plan and strategy, and my love of property investment. The biggest and best change has been my relationship with Katrina. We are an awesome team; we have similar mindsets and also spiritual beliefs about life in general and we work amazingly well together. We have great synergy together and do a lot more combined than we would ever do as individuals. Synergy means 'one plus one equals three'. She has helped me find my passion for real estate in a new way and I enjoy every day we spend together, whether it's doing real estate deals together or away somewhere on holiday. Without Katrina, I wouldn't have bought the 20 rental properties in one year in 2014 or written this book, nor would I have helped the HB investors for 12 months running seminars and coaching them with their property investing. I also wouldn't have had as much fun, love and laughter every day as I do now. Every day brings something new and exciting, and life is now like one big long holiday that doesn't ever end.

Since March 2013 when Katrina moved in with me, I've bought around 80 properties in a little over three years. Some of these were sold on to other investors, and many were renovated and sold again. The rest have been held onto as long term rental properties. The profit from the trades/renovation properties over the last three years has averaged out at approximately $300,000 each year. The rents I get from all the *rental* properties (62 out of a total of around 72 properties) including one commercial property is nearly $20,000 a week, or just over $1 million per year. Expenses such as rates, insurance, maintenance, property management and the mortgages all come out of this every month, and leave a cash-flow after all expenses of $170,000 a year. This will increase to over $250,000 within the next 18 months as the higher interest rate loans come off their fixed rates, as long as interest rates stay close to where they are now in the low 4%p.a. area. Also nearly $25,000 each month is paid down in principal off my overall loan balance. Each month the amount getting paid down in principal increases slightly, as happens with all P & I loans. Near the end of the loans this will increase to around $50,000 a month being paid off these loans as *more* principal gets paid off and *less* interest.

You will read in a couple of the articles coming up soon called 'Building a Solid Foundation in Real Estate'. These are really important articles to read and to understand. Without a good solid foundation, you could easily end up losing everything like so many other investors have done in the past, with only a very slight drop in market prices. My foundation now I believe is very solid and it gets stronger each month as more equity is gained in the properties. The LVR on my properties has recently gone below 50% (meaning I own more than I owe) and is slowly going down each month and will continue to do so until all the loans are paid off in full.

Please read the Foreword by Mike Russell, the entertaining story of Katrina's journey at the beginning of Part 2, and all the articles, *before* moving on to the remainder of this book. Part 3 is where the focus then moves on to buying the 20 rental properties using no equity that I purchased in 2014. It's a bit like building a foundation in real estate; you need to build that first.

As mentioned earlier the introduction and all the other parts of this book are building a solid foundation to your *knowledge*, and by reading all of this first, you will get so much more out of the book.

Thank you.
Graeme Fowler

FOREWORD

The only thing that went worse than the first meeting with Graeme Fowler, was my second meeting.

At the time, I was a captain at Air New Zealand, and also on the executive committee of the Hawkes Bay Property Investors' Association and I had been investing in property for about six years.

Graeme was attending the AGM of the Hawkes Bay Property Investors' Association and I happened to be giving a presentation on two properties we had purchased earlier in the year. The two properties were ex-state houses, one with a lot of damage. This had bought our property portfolio to a total of four properties at the time. It was at this meeting, when my wife asked a question on property valuations and capital gains, that Graeme thought we really needed help. The next day he invited us to join his free 12 month mentoring group he was about to start, along with other Hawkes Bay investors, meeting monthly in Havelock North. We had been seeking out a mentor for a while and had already spent some money on personal development. I had also completed a Dale Carnegie course, which on reflection blew the doors wide open for opportunity.

During the first group meeting with Graeme speaking to about 40 keen property investors, he offered the investors to meet up with him for a coffee and a chat, so I jumped at the chance.

I met with him first; we had a general chat about what we were doing, how it was going, and the thing that struck me was that he was really interested and kept asking questions like "why are you doing it this way, why are you thinking that way?" I was starting to become frustrated as previous mentors hadn't asked me these tough questions. I also realised that I hadn't previously asked these tough questions of *myself*.

Graeme suggested I bring some more detailed information and my wife Steph along to the next one on one meeting, great I thought!

Second meeting, we had some facts and figures, but it didn't get off to a good start. At that time in our property portfolio, we had five properties, two in Havelock North, the jewels in the crown I thought, and three in Hastings. Within two minutes, Graeme had put crosses through both of the Havelock North properties and gave the tick of approval for two of the Hastings properties, giving the third, a maybe. I couldn't believe it, he told me the Havelock North properties were only yielding 5%, and they were holding us back. Then he looked over the loan structure, it got worse. He was asking what loan was assigned to what house, and what each house was costing us. I didn't have all the answers. Graeme leaned forward with head in his hands, shaking his head from side to side. He couldn't make sense of my information. We walked out of the meeting, I was angry, my wife burst into tears in the car, and I remembered saying, "what the hell does he know about property anyway?!" Turns out, quite a bit!

Graeme had shined a light on our property portfolio and the foundation was very shaky. Our property structure looked like a big bucket that you tip money into the top of, and there's a hole in the bottom, only we didn't know how big that hole was, and how much we were losing.

I was and still am, amazed that the detail Graeme went into looking at our properties. In his own portfolio, he knows at any given second, where he stands financially and what his rentals are costing and returning.

Lesson number one: know the numbers.

Lesson number two was about the 'mind' and this was introduced to us by Graeme, through Abraham Hicks. Graeme used to go to monthly meetings and asked me if I wanted to come along one evening. The best way to describe Abraham Hicks is that it alerts you to the power of your mind, and what you *think* has everything to do with what you *receive* in life. Esther is the medium for Abraham and she has a great way of translating complicated concepts into very simple terms. So as I went along to more of these meetings, I realised that *I'm* responsible for everything that happens to me. I am in control. I quickly realised 'Mike, you need to get in the driving seat, drive, and also enjoy the journey'.

So at that second meeting, the journey with Graeme had started. All it had cost me so far was $9.00 for two peppermint teas with honey, and my time.

Over the next two years, we sold our two Havelock North properties and I got the opportunity I had always planned for, to finish flying for Air NZ and work full time in property, somewhat sooner than I had thought. At the time Air NZ was restructuring the domestic bases in New Zealand and the Napier base was the first to be reviewed, the result being impending base closure within 24 months. I opted to retire from flying commercially, leaving Air NZ, taking the exit package and cashing in my superannuation policy. Steph went back to work full-time and took up a technical position in the Pip-fruit industry. This was an industry she had left seven years prior, to start our family. So my new job was 'property investor' and 'stay at home Dad' to our son Max, who was seven at the time.

Shortly thereafter, I successfully got appointed as the President of the Hawkes Bay Property Investors' Association (HBPIA). Looking back at all that was going on, I had taken on too much. I made a tough call to step down after only six months in the job as President. It was a decision I didn't take lightly. I had been on the executive committee for four years prior, and found the HBPIA was a great way to learn, network and meet fellow property investors. I am still a member and attend the monthly meetings when I can.

Graeme continued the mentoring sessions for 12 months as promised, and we also had regular catch ups with Graeme over a peppermint tea. I also walked the goat track up Te Mata Peak with Graeme many times. Exercise is a great way to clear the mind. Over this period we learnt so much about property investing, with one common thread, being Graeme's honesty about our situation. He continued to ask 'WHY?' I also learnt to ask *better* questions of Graeme, the more thought you put into a question, the better the answer you would always get. This point was made even clearer to me after reading a book that Graeme had suggested I read, "Wink and Grow Rich" by Roger Hamilton.

As we bought more properties, we could bounce ideas off Graeme, asking questions all the time. We started buying properties that yielded 10% and formed a great relationship with a local property manager. Problems started disappearing left, right and centre. We were reducing our debt levels, money started to flow in and we finally had control of our property portfolio. So our current portfolio details are an LVR approaching 60%, cash-flow positive, and eight investment properties. This does not include our own home. We plan on continuing to grow our portfolio.

My journey with property has been greatly enhanced by three key factors, Graeme Fowler's mentorship, the Dale Carnegie training and the teachings of Abraham Hicks.

If I was to summarise my mindset about property now, it would be:

- We have a very clear reason *why* we are involved in property investing. That being simply an income to allow us an early retirement.
- Graeme has taught us to take the emotions out of our decisions, thus reducing our stress levels and therefore making better decisions.
- Property is fun! When you enjoy something, you do a better job at it.

Please enjoy this book. I hope the insights help you with your property investing journey, like it has with ours.

Finally, what I admire about Graeme is, he's not afraid to ask the questions, but more than that, he's not afraid of the answers.

So thank you Graeme for all the help and honest advice you have given us, we are truly grateful.

Mike Russell.

THE 'WHAT'S SO' ABOUT 'WHAT'S SO'.

'What's so' is always just 'what's so'.

'What's so' doesn't care what you think, feel, intend or wish; it will not bend.

You can be freaked out by 'what's so', and it won't change 'what's so'.

If you're late for an appointment, getting annoyed, upset, worried or angry about it won't get you there any earlier.

If you're having a bad day, being freaked out or upset about it won't change 'what's so'.

That which you seek will not bring you satisfaction – aligning with 'what's so', will.

When you're upset, you're never upset about 'what's so'.

'What's so' is just 'what's so', and you're upset.

'What's so' doesn't care if you're upset, it's up to you to handle 'what's so'.

There is no confusion in 'what's so'.

When you don't know, you just don't know – there's no confusion there.

There's nothing right or wrong about 'what's so'.

'What's so' is always open to different interpretations.

There's always just 'what's so', and you have an *interpretation* about it.

'What's so' doesn't scare you, it's your interpretation of 'what's so' that scares you.

The interpretation is never true; 'what's so' is real, the interpretation is not.

Who you're being is just who you're being, and 'what's so' doesn't care if you're happy with it or not.

So why should you?

When you're not being with 'what's so', that's also just 'what's so'.

Why should you concern yourself?

Other people are always being the way they are being; if you think they shouldn't be that way, that's your interpretation.

Bring yourself back to 'what's' so about them.

Until you can be with 'what's so', you can't be with anything, or anyone.

You may have control or influence over other people's 'what's so', but none over their interpretation, so give it up.

If you take action or you don't take action, it's just 'what's so'.

If it works out well or not, it's still just 'what's so'.

You can never make a right or wrong decision, or take a right or wrong action.

Whatever you do will just bring you *more* of 'what's so', and then you have an interpretation about it.

Whatever you don't have, so what?

Whatever you've done or thought in the past, it's just 'what's so'.

Whatever happens in the future is not to be feared, it's just going to more of 'what's so'.

The challenge is to spend as much time in 'what's so' as you can.

The chatter in your head is more interpretation, and it has nothing to do with 'what's so'.

There's nothing wrong with the chatter, it's just you listening to a fantasy.

The thought that there's something wrong is an illusion; there is nothing wrong, there is only 'what's so'.

Notice when you're comparing 'what's so' to some fantasy of how you think it should be.

Bring yourself back to 'what's so' and it will be okay.

Ask yourself 'what's so', and align with that.

Align with 'what's so' and it will not matter.

That is the foundation of transformation and satisfaction.

Not aligning with 'what's so' is the only thing that will ever bring you hardship.

Life in '*what's so*' will bring you peace, harmony, grace and balance.

Ask yourself; 'what's so' about *your* situation?

PART 1.

Article

'Who Benefits?'

by Graeme Fowler written in 2002.

Both of the quotes below are from a couple of newspapers during the week.

"Real Estate Institute president Graeme Woodley said people should buy now because prices were not going to fall. All indicators pointed toward the continuing strength of the market, with continued positive migration, a healthy economy and low unemployment."

And this one: –

"Such a rapid rate of building in the face of slowing demand is a recipe for an oversupplied housing market and, consequently, falling house prices. While house prices are likely to climb further over the next six months, Infometrics predicts that property values will begin to fall before the end of this year."

One says you should buy now because prices are not going to fall. The other one predicts that house prices will fall by the end of this year. Who's correct? Are either of them correct? Who knows for sure? I have said this many, many times to property investors before, that no one really knows what will happen in the market from one day to the next. I often get people ask me what I think prices will do, it can sometimes sounds like a broken record. Naturally, I don't know any more than the next person does. But people assume because of my involvement in property that I must also be able to predict future market trends and prices – which obviously I cannot do, much to their amazement. Although many people claim to be able to do this with an array of often confusing & baffling data, historic statistics and other jargon, I am yet to meet anyone that can consistently predict market trends accurately. Even if there was such an enlightened individual, it would not be a given that their predictions would continue to be accurate anytime in the future. One thing to keep in mind is that whenever you hear any advice, opinions or see any articles written like, or similar to the ones below – always, always keep this in mind, and ask yourself: – "WHO BENEFITS???"

An agent that wants to sell more houses may tell their buyers that house prices are going to 'keep going through the roof" and if you don't buy now, you are an imbecile and will miss out on all those capital gains, 'you would be crazy not to buy now'. He may also tell his vendors that now is a great time to sell because you can lock in all those capital gains that you have achieved since buying your home, 'if you hold on too long, you could lose all what you've gained.' A mortgage broker may also tell their investor clients to buy more investment properties because prices will continue to rise, with the appropriate evidence to back it up. An insurance salesperson may on the other hand tell prospective clients that the market is about to turn bad and this could also affect businesses and no doubt employment (of course with solid evidence to support it) and hence want to sell their clients income protection insurance – after all, they could be made redundant. Investors themselves may even tell others and endeavour to spread the word that property prices will soon become stagnant or even come down, in the hope that what they are saying will have an effect in some small way. This would help them to buy properties once again at cheaper more affordable prices. It may seem odd to say or even think this, but if no one really knows for sure what the future holds, ask yourself – why would they be telling me this? Do they have their own agenda attached to what they are saying in any way? Other people may use their predictions and assumptions to sell their books, seminars, magazines, website services, publications, subscriptions or other information they have available, or even for simply the sake of being 'right' – as many economists will do. In another local newspaper I saw on the same day as the two excerpts above, five economists predicted the official cash rate would rise in January, seven said it would rise in March, and one said it wouldn't be raised now until June.

It is not always the case that the person or organisation behind these types of market predictions has their own best interests at heart. But, simply ask yourself before you take it as gospel that what they are saying is based on sound logic, reasoning, and a likelihood of being true; – is this information or advice in any way *benefiting* the author(s) of the material, and therefore the theories and opinions behind the information biased in *any* way? Is what they are telling me endeavouring to convince me to *buy* something from them, or change the ways I currently act or do things? Who benefits *the most* if I act upon what they are saying? What do *they* get out of it if I believe them, or if their predictions come true?

Always ask yourself this – who benefits the most if they persuade me to *believe* them??

Article

'Getting Into Line'

by Graeme Fowler written in 2004.

"Get into a line that you will find to be a deep personal interest, something that you really enjoy spending 12 - 15 hours a day working at, and the rest of the time thinking about". Earl Nightingale.

Above is one of the quotes I have used in my book. I think for the people starting out in real estate, in business, or any profession for that matter, it's important to really understand this quote. Too many people are looking for a quick fix, or the one answer or idea that is going to be the secret to making them rich. While this can happen, it is rare and your chances of winning Lotto may be a better bet.

Think of it this way: – let's say you're standing in line at a lunch bar with a big line of people standing there waiting to be fed. It's the only lunch bar in town with all the types of food that you want to eat at. You join the line at the back of the queue where everyone else joins, and the queue seems to go on and on for as far as you can see, and you're hungry. While you're standing there, it seems as if the queue has stopped and you're getting nowhere, but eventually it moves for a short time, before it once again comes to a complete stop. All this time you're waiting in line, you're not eating and you're getting more and more frustrated, upset and hungry. If you get tired of waiting and decide to jump out of line for a break, you'll then need to join once again at the back of the queue, and start all over again. When you re-join the line, there may even be more people in line than there was before. By trying to jump in front of other people or push in, you are only going to upset the others around you and be told to join the queue at the end of the line once more. Only by staying in line for the amount of time *you need to*, will you ever get the food, and of course be able to eat.

Think of the food at the end of the line as being the money you want to earn in real estate or in business. Something that you are passionate about doing in your life, something that may be a tremendous challenge for you to achieve. For example, you may decide you want to be a successful long-term buy and hold real estate investor with a passive income of $1,000 a week within the next 20 - 25 years. But within a short while of beginning, if you go off on another tangent to pursue something else, you are jumping *out of line*. You might have the thought that lease-options are now the way to go instead, or that building spec houses, relocating houses, or investing in the share market or even commercial property is a better and more exciting way for you now. So you decide to sell your rental properties, and give up your place in line. Only by staying in line long enough will you get to reach your goals and be able to eat. By jumping out of line constantly, in other words, getting side-tracked and going off in other directions and doing something else, you will lose your place in line, and never reach the front of the line to get fed.

It is similar with your team of professionals you work with; – such as real estate salespeople, lawyers, accountants, banks, trades-people and even mentors. You may have to stand in line for quite some time, getting more and more upset, annoyed and frustrated, and seemingly getting nowhere with the people you are currently associated with or working with, before eventually the right people show up that can help you speed up the process, understand what you are wanting to achieve, and make the journey more pleasant and comfortable. It took me five years or so to get the best people in each of these areas that I was happy working with. But I had to stay in line *waiting* for these people to show up.

So in summary, learn how to stay in line for the amount of time that's necessary in order to be fed. Once you make up your mind about the goals you want to achieve in life and written them down, stay with it, stay with it, stay with it, *especially* when the going gets tough. Make *perseverance, patience and vision* the words that you hang on the wall where you can see them every day.

Others may also be finding it hard going, and be willing to give up their place in line for you.

Article

'Tempted by a Booming Market?'

by Graeme Fowler written in 2004.

A few days ago, a man walked into my office wanting to talk about investing in New Zealand Real Estate. Apparently, he had just visited one of the real estate companies in town, and they had suggested he come and talk to me for some investment advice. This is how the conversation went:

Investor: I was told you might be able to help me with some projections.
Graeme: Okay, what sort of projections are you after?
Investor: On real estate prices over the next five years.
Graeme: I'm not sure what you mean by projections, can you explain please?
Investor: Well, I have a group of investors that have some money to invest, and we want to buy some properties together as an investment. I need to be able to tell them how much we can make, and what sort of returns we are likely to get in five years from now. Can you help with some projections on prices?
Graeme: So, you mean you want me to tell you what *prices* will be in five years time, compared to what they are now?
Investor: Yes please, that is what I am after.
Graeme: I have no idea what prices will be in five years time, two years time, or even this time next year. I would only be guessing, as would anybody else you ask. In fact, this is one of the major reasons why people lose money investing in property; they go into it for the wrong reasons, hoping that the properties they buy always go up in value. Then when they don't go up, or they drop in value, they get despondent and sell. I have written a book about real estate investment that explains about this. You would be better to read it before doing anything else, especially if you are investing money for *other* people. Would you like a copy to read?
Investor: No, I don't want to read a book; I just want to invest some money in real estate because I've been told it's a good investment.
Graeme: Well good luck, but I'm sorry, I cannot help you with what you're after.

I was at first stunned by what this guy was wanting, but on reflection, realised there are probably many other investors just like him. They hear real estate values are going up, so they rush in to buy something without any knowledge of what they are doing. I don't ever try to predict what is going to happen in the market, but if I *were* to guess what will happen, it would be that the market will start to change soon, especially when *people like this* are starting to become real estate investors.

I remember at one of the Hawkes Bay Property Investors' Association meetings I attended back in early 2000, everyone at the meeting was fairly despondent about the real estate market. I think I was one of the only people that put my hand up at the meeting when they asked who was looking at buying more properties during that year. The majority of people were either holding what they had, or selling. It was recommended by the President at the time, plus a few elderly investors, that a cautious approach should be taken, and not to take on any more debt because there was so much pessimism with the market. They were saying that house prices were far too high, the market was at a peak and perhaps even to sell one or two properties if they had a larger portfolio. I said to my friend Richard who was sitting next to me at the time – 'that's it, I'm going to buy as much as I can this year!' I ended up buying 28 properties that year and 32 the following year. The majority of people were pessimistic, and I was buying everything I could.

Having said that, when I buy any property, it must make sense to me at the time of purchasing, not only make sense if the market increases by some fictitious amount year after year. It seems with both real estate and shares, when the market is rising, everyone wants to get in, and when the market is falling, everyone is running away from it. If your favourite supermarket started to put all its prices up, you would walk away from it, just as you would buy more from them if they were having a big sale. Investing in real estate is no different, but people do the exact opposite to what they would do when buying everyday products.

If you are just beginning to invest in real estate, think carefully. Are you doing it simply because it seems like the popular thing to do and all your friends are doing it? Take a long term approach before you do anything, get some advice or opinions from people that have been successful, not in just up-markets, but over a long term. Also, use a mentor if you think it would help, and keep developing your own positive mindset and psychology.

Article

'What's the Property Market Doing, and Should it Really Matter?'

by Graeme Fowler written in March 2005.

Perhaps the most common question I get asked as a property investor is 'what do you think the market is going to do?' I will usually answer with something like 'I have no idea what will happen, and I really don't care'. A couple of months ago I was invited along to a free two hour seminar put on by one of the major banks on property investment. The guy that was speaking had one property himself which he was now selling as he thought it was a good time to sell. The rest of the time was spent going through a whole range of meaningless graphs, charts, facts and figures explaining to us all what he thought *might* happen to property prices over the next few years. Of course he really had no idea and admitted that many things could affect what he thought might possibly happen anyway. It's extremely tiresome to me hearing about, or reading about peoples' opinions in newspapers or magazine articles, about what they *think* property prices will do. The fact is, nobody *really* ever knows what will happen, and more importantly – *why* should it matter anyway?! It matters very little to me whether prices rise, fall or even stay the same for the next 20 years or more. By having investing rules that work whatever happens to property prices is one of the keys to successful investing.

P&I vs Interest Only

Most investors use the traditional 'buy and hold' as their main strategy which is fine.

There are also those investors that use buy and hold as one strategy, and also use one or a number of other methods including; – trading, renovating and reselling, lease-options, developing, or building. I use the 'buy and hold', 'renovations', and the 'trading' strategies. Now, if you have an investor that just uses the 'buy and hold' strategy and has been investing for a few years, should it matter if the market price of their properties goes up or down in value from time to time over the next 20 - 40 years? The answer of course is no. But what *makes* it matter to them is when they decide to use 'interest only' loans, as opposed to P & I loans. Now they are forever hoping, maybe even praying – for ever increasing prices.

New investors will often ask 'is now a good time to buy, or do you think I should wait until the market goes down a bit (or crashes)?' One of the biggest problems I see with property investment is that people go into it for the wrong reasons, or with their own *assumptions* – and not even knowing they *are* assumptions.

The biggest assumption of all is that 'property will always go up in value'. The majority of investors rely on future capital gains before they make any real money. Starting with the assumption that prices will forever keep going up, many people decide to finance their properties using an interest only loan as opposed to a P & I loan. With an interest only loan, you do get a few dollars extra a week in cash-flow, but the property *never* gets paid off unless you pay for it from somewhere else. The investor relies on their rental property going up in value perpetually, thereby gaining more equity in the property, which they often take out by refinancing, and then buying further properties. This now takes them back up to a similar LVR ratio as when they first bought the property. This can go on as long as they continue to invest in property, forever refinancing when prices go up and always being heavily geared. To me, this is such a dangerous strategy and one I'm personally heavily against.

If they truly are a 'buy and hold' investor for the long term, I will often ask these investors if they think there is any possibility of prices dropping by 15 - 20% *anytime* over the next 30 or so years? Of course the answer is that it is possible and it's already happened in many other countries in the past including the U.S. and Japan. So, if there is always this possibility, why would they risk *all* they own on it not happening? All that would need to happen is that you are geared at 80 - 90% over your entire property portfolio say in 10 or 15 years time, and the property market then suddenly slumps 20% within a year. This could happen for any number of reasons including interest rate rises, a change in government or banking policies, war, world-wide share market crash, an outbreak of foot and mouth disease in NZ, baby boomers retiring etc, etc. Now, because of the reduced equity in your property portfolio, your bank manager wants you to come up with at least $200,000 by the end of the month, as he considers you are too highly geared and too much of a risk for their bank. You can't even sell these properties now for what the mortgage is on them, so you're forced into bankruptcy unless you can come up with the necessary cash to reduce your LVR.

Property investment can be so simple, and I think because it is so simple, most people want to complicate it, and end up losing money long term. With investment in property, business or shares, the majority of investors lose *long term*. Any investor can make money, or think they are doing well in a rising market, but will their rules and strategies work equally as well in a down-trending market? Most of the time, the answer is no.

Are You Creating Wealth, or Protecting it?

I think before getting into property investment at all, people need to ask themselves the question; – do I want to do this for 'wealth creation', or do I want to do it for 'wealth retention?'

The 'buy and hold' strategy is used mainly for 'wealth retention' and I think where a lot of investors go wrong is they try to use it for their 'wealth creation' vehicle. A business owner or an employee with a reasonable income could use his/her savings for deposits on rental properties, even if it's just one or two a year over the next 10 years. The tenants end up paying off the loans on these properties over the following 20 - 25 years *(N.B. the investor of course needs as one of his/her rules a gross yield that is acceptable before purchasing any rental property)*. This also acts as *very slow* 'wealth creation', as the tenants eventually pay the loans off (on P & I) in full, but it's actually a 'wealth retention' method. A trader, renovator or developer has the intention of making *quick cash* profits which is a 'wealth creation' method, or strategy. They may then use the income from this to park into property, which then turns it into 'wealth retention'. Where the thinking goes wrong with many investors is they try to use a 'buy and hold' (wealth retention) strategy with their properties as a '*wealth creation*' vehicle. Often these property investors will talk about wanting a small *positive cash–flow* from a huge number of properties in order to replace their current income from a job, or to enable them to sell their business. They want to use a 'wealth retention' method for the purpose of 'wealth creation'. This one distinction if not fully understood, could well lead to the downfall of many property investors over the next ten to fifteen years.

Do You Have a Passion For Property?

From the nearly 15 years of experience I've had in real estate investing, I've noticed that the investors who have a *passion* for property investing will often use *other* strategies in real estate such as property trading, renovations, lease-options, writing books, doing seminars, or mentoring others, to help with their own 'wealth creation'. Therefore, these investors can have *multiple* streams of income from one solid base, which is property. And those investors that have property as more of an *interest* to them, rather than it being a passion to them, use property as a 'wealth retention' tool. The problem as mentioned is when many of these investors try to use the 'buy and hold' strategy as a 'wealth creation' vehicle (instead of 'wealth retention') to replace their income from a job or a business they don't enjoy being at. I think a lot of this way of thinking has been created after people have read books like 'RichDad PoorDad' or 'Cashflow Quadrant', and then thinking they must be in the 'ratrace'. They also want to be a 'Business Owner' or an 'Investor', not just an 'Employee' or a 'Self Employed'. The point to realise is that the wealthiest people in the world today *still* go to work, even though they *don't have to* – because they have a passion for what they do. They *love* their work, they don't want to be doing anything else! And at the end of the day they are still an *'Employee'* as well as a 'Business Owner' or 'Investor'.

Summary

So, what are my answers to the previous questions – 'what do you think the market is going to do?' and 'is now a good time to buy, or do you think I should wait until the market goes down?' My answer is simple – 'start asking *better* questions! ☺

PART 2.

My partner Katrina, her story and how she got started in Property.

I couldn't believe how lucky I was to have someone famous coming to my house, NZ's number one best-selling author on property, business man and multi-millionaire, Graeme Fowler was on his way. As I watched the lights of his black WRX 555 turn into my drive, I could barely contain my nerves. He had an incredibly strong hand-shake (wow I touched him) was about all I could think about for the first several minutes as I showed him around my property. I didn't know whether to sit, stand, or jump up and down as my excitement and nerves boiled over. He was now sitting at my table eye-balling me with his intensely deep questions, and while I knew the answers, today it was like my memory had been wiped. Control, alt, deleted! Blank screen. I was like a rabbit in headlights. Then a turning point happened, Graeme pulled out a hankie and blew his nose and said 'just getting over a cold', and from that point on I realised he was like everyone else, he also got colds! Unbelievable, we had something in common.

Some of my first impressions of Graeme were an incredible ability to do calculations in his head, he was approachable, had a quirky sense of humour, was very calm, and he always left you thinking for yourself. It was almost like a marketing campaign where you had to go back the next day and see if you had all the answers right, and get your next clues. Except this wasn't a game, it was my financial situation, my mindset and my entire self worth.

This was (not that I knew it at the time) the beginning of a massive turning point in my very safe, predictable, and up until now, normal life. I completed a degree at Massey, had been married for 12 years, had three kids, and owned a plum orchard on the outskirts of Havelock

North. I enjoyed real estate, and my husband and I had done well with our own homes, prior to moving to Hawkes Bay. This meant we owned a half share of a 10 acre orchard with my parents. We built two new houses on the land for additional income. There was already an original 1960's house situated on the property, alongside income from the orchard lease. Looking back now our mortgage was small and safe, although it didn't seem small at the time. So when my parents decided they wanted to sell their half share of the property and move out of the area, we put the orchard on the market. It was listed for $1.1 million and we started looking for a house to buy in town. After quickly realising that life in town wasn't going to work for us, my husband said 'why don't we buy your parents out?' He wanted to keep the orchard. This sent shivers up my spine because at the same time we had an offer presented to us for $1 million, and my parents wanted to accept it. In our relationship I was in charge of the financial situation. And while our relationship overall was very even; Dennis didn't deal with banks, lending, or make any decisions regarding money, I did it all. So here I am faced with my parents wanting out, and my husband determined not to sell. We needed to find $500,000 immediately in order to stay. For the first time in my life I felt overwhelmed, confused and stuck. I had enormous pressure to make a decision and one stubborn husband who wasn't prepared to move. This was causing a lot of conflict and strain on my husband's relationship with my parents.

Then into my life strolls Graeme Fowler. Like winning the power-ball in lotto, unbelievable timing. How lucky was I?!! So this is how he ended up at my table, eye-balling me.

Graeme was very quick to say that buying out my parents was the best way forward. He gave me sound reasoning, solid financial solutions, reassurance and support. Not only that, but he gave me three options on buying out my parents that I had never even considered. Graeme quickly became my sounding board as I went through this process, I would text him and say I hadn't slept all night from worrying, and he would offer to chat over the phone or a cuppa. However I wasn't an over the phone talker, so I followed him up Te Mata Peak as I knew he walked it daily. Graeme is very structured, disciplined and very routine. Three characteristics I definitely wasn't! But I was fast becoming aware of the importance of all these things in Graeme's life.

So here I am on a massive learning journey towards what Graeme talks about as financial intelligence, gathering up a team as I go along; mortgage brokers, accountants, lawyers, valuers, bank managers, tradespeople and property managers. And now on top of all that, I felt like Sir Edmund Hillary conquering a massive mountain each day in order to have Graeme's full attention, away from all of the day's interruptions. Then I would follow him home if I wasn't finished with all my questions, or I would show up before picking my kids up from school, so it wasn't long before he knew exactly how I liked my coffee.

What attracted me the most about Graeme was his advice, support, and his opinions always felt right. It was safe and well supported and Graeme had proved it all worked, he believed in building a solid foundation before anything else. So he taught me about LVRs, yields, the power of leverage, compounding interest, negotiations (which I still suck at) and also, and more important than anything, he taught me about the 'Law of Attraction'. What I think, say, and feel is a direct reflection back on what is happening in my life, at any point in time. And yes this meant many, many, intense conversations up Te Mata Peak, as I figured out how this Law of Attraction all worked.

So skipping ahead a few years and here I am now living with Graeme (as you would have read in the intro) and Graeme decides to try out this idea of buying 10 houses with one deposit. I was very excited and eager to see Graeme in action, because up until now I had only read about his ability to buy houses in his book. I often doubted him, and used to have him on about not being the successful person he made out to be in his book! Since I had met him, the only thing he was really interested in was finding a relationship (another book in itself), so this was my opportunity to hopefully learn from a real master in property investment.

I said to him 'what if I use the equity from the orchard (in partnership with my ex) and do the same thing with your help?' So off we go. Well it was like Usain Bolt vs a toddler learning to walk. Graeme's years of financial intelligence, team building, knowledge and skills really were incredible, and I was such a beginner. I had limited time (as I was working and raising three children), I had no negotiation skills, I was never in the right place at the right time, I had no confidence in working with a mortgage broker to explain what I wanted to do, and real estate salespeople were frustrating me with their slackness. It was hard for me not to feel jealous and frustrated when Graeme would tell me about the property with an 11% yield he'd just bought. However one thing I had worked on a lot over the past few years was my own personal development, and my (now) strong understanding of the 'Law of Attraction', especially the teachings of Abraham Hicks. So I knew jealously, frustrations and excuses were things that I had created, and so couldn't use Graeme as my excuse as to why I was feeling these things. I was the problem, nothing else and nobody else. I knew I had to change my mindset and my own beliefs that I could do this. Also that I deserved it, and everything is always working out perfectly for me, no matter how it appears at any given time. Because in life, there really isn't any 'right and wrong', or 'good and bad'. In life, 'you can't get it wrong and you can never get it all done'. So enjoy the journey, have fun and be happy. Using other people as your excuse only gives them the power to control your happiness.

Once I relaxed and started to visualise what my house/s might look like, I created a vision board and felt excited about even the possibility of being a property investor. Things then started to change; my brother-in-law rang to say his uncle wanted to sell his house in Flaxmere and asked me if I would be interested in buying it. Before I knew it I had six houses within a very short period of time. Five of these were private sales and one through a local real estate agent. Apart from the first purchase, all the properties I bought were through Graeme's network and contacts.

In this book you will read all the articles that have helped me learn and build up my own portfolio and foundation. Graeme has an incredible gift in this industry and is passionate about sharing his learnings, experience, and wealth of knowledge, with anyone that wants to learn. How you choose to use this information to start, or expand your own portfolio is entirely up to you, but don't use other people as your excuse for not being proactive. Coming up with a plan and some goals for your future costs you nothing but your time. Understanding all of this is a key building block to your wealth.

You will also find an article coming up soon in this book that I wrote about my six investment properties from a beginners view point, which is an entirely different journey to Graeme's. I have also started up a

Facebook group called "Women in Property Investing NZ" which is focused on helping to inspire, motivate and encourage women to invest in property. So please find the link below and ask to join. I know both Hawkes Bay and Auckland ladies have regular coffee days where we can catch up and talk with like-minded women.

https://www.facebook.com/groups/1791590287729377/

So where to now for me? In June 2016 I left my job and became a full-time property investor. Sounds pretty easy, right?! I mean I live with Graeme Fowler so what could possibility go wrong? In the past, friends and family have often made comments to us like 'oh, you still send Katrina out to work each day', or 'you're rich, why does Katrina need to work?', or 'how come you aren't paying for her holiday?' While I understand that they all mean well – what annoys me most is that the assumption that because Graeme is wealthy and successful, that he should automatically support his partner in life. I mean 'why would I need to build and grow my own wealth if Graeme has enough money for us both?'

Simple. It's my life and I get to choose exactly how it's played out! Why would I choose to live with someone successful and knowledgeable in their industry, and not learn how it's done?! I get to have the control and power of my decisions every day, and I don't hold anyone else accountable for my life or my happiness. I don't even ask my ex-husband for money for our children because I chose to have three children, and I will provide for them. If he chooses to pay me money, I see this as a bonus. But I will never rely on it to support us, as it always has the possibility of leading to disappointment in one form or another. And at times it's been really tough for me, especially going from two incomes (when I was married) down to only mine. But I had the control and the power to change it, and make the most of the situation. As a result I am very close to my ex; we have a wonderful relationship which is fantastic for the children, and far more beneficial than fighting over child support.

However, one of the hardest things I found with being independent is the ability to depend, or lean on others, and to help grow myself. And this was exactly what I was faced with a few months ago when Graeme offered to help me with leaving my job. He offered me, what could be the biggest opportunity in my entire life. To leave work and do property full-time. This was my dream; it was what I had laid in bed thinking about my entire life, being an independent and successful woman. So why did something feel off? It was entirely my own mindset. I am first and foremost a Mum of three very dependent children, and I have a mortgage (with the house I own with Graeme). So it seemed ridiculous to give up the security of a job that I had worked for my entire life, and take the huge risk of trading houses full-time. It's okay for a man, he has no responsibilities like some women do, it's easier for men to get jobs and it's easier for them to get back on their feet. All excuses for me to stay in my safe place, in my secure job and have my six rental houses! But I wanted more. I wanted to be my own boss, and also knew that I was worth more than the $34 per hour that the government was paying me in my job. So after a few weeks I decided to take Graeme up on his offer and hand in my notice at work! Wow I felt great – I no longer hated Mondays and I was enjoying the possibilities that were arising. I had several job offers (not that I considered taking any of them) and I also applied to be a Marriage Celebrant, as this was something I had always wanted to do. Everything was falling nicely into place and I was enjoying the adventure as I went along. I must admit though that the last week of my job was very tough. The realisation hit me of 'no turning back now', but the minute I walked out the door on my last day at work, it was an instant feeling of freedom!

So today, here I am; ready to go up Te Mata peak with Graeme for our morning walk, and then later put house number three on the market. I have a child who has gone to school not feeling that well, but know that I'm around if she needs to be picked up from school early. It's great being around for times like this when one of the kids might get sick and need a day off school, and not have to go to work to keep my boss happy!

I'm enjoying my relationship with Graeme way more than I thought I would, we seem to have fantastic energy and drive in everything we do together. Our houses turn out way better than if we were doing them individually, and we go together like 'copy and paste'. I have also come to realise that I can still be an independent successful person, alongside another human that shares the same passion and values as I do. Neither of us needs each other in order to be happy or successful, but instead we want each other, and this is what makes it so perfect.

In summary I would say property investing is much like the first time I walked up Te Mata peak, totally unprepared for the conditions ahead. It was a hot sunny day; I had no water, was really unfit, and was still getting over a head-cold. I also hadn't even realised that we were walking up a mountain. I also thought because I was with someone who was experienced, I would be fine. As it turned out, I ended up laying down flat on the side of a hill, dehydrated and feeling like I needed to vomit. I didn't want to continue up the hill but had come too far to turn back now. I really wanted someone to fly in with a helicopter and rescue me. Many people walked past and offered me their support and encouragement, but no one offered to carry me. I had to get there one way or another, on my own. Graeme eventually came looking for me and showed me a few short cuts to get to the top, but still only I could do it. By this time I was sore, tired and angry, and blamed the whole situation on Graeme. He knew exactly how hard it was, he never showed me the much easier track to begin with, or even suggest that I should take water! I soon realised though that I was only upset and annoyed at myself for not being prepared, being unfit, and also naive to the entire situation. Not only that, how could Graeme have known my fitness level? He was kind enough to show me the walking track and support me, plus I took up an extra half hour of his day while he waited for me at the top. He never walked off or got annoyed at my lack of preparedness. He just said 'next time will be a lot easier!' ☺

The following day I was still sore and somewhat frustrated, however I decided to go back up again, but this time do a slightly easier and shorter route. I built up my fitness a few more times on the easier track, and then within a week I took on the almighty goat track once again, this time with a lot more knowledge and experience. I now walk Te Mata peak regularly and have continued to do so since those early days. Some days it's still really tough, and other days it's a bit easier, but I know the reward at the top is worth it. Not just the stunning views and the sense of achievement, but also for my overall health and well being. I am confident and know my limits, so I know exactly when I can push myself hard, and also when to take it easy.

This turns out to be very similar to property investing. If you don't have a plan or a route to follow, you may want to rush ahead because everyone else is doing it. However, without first getting a sound understanding of how, and more importantly 'why' you are doing it, then you too are likely to get stranded on your back, not knowing where to go, or what to do next. And guess what? Nobody is going to save you (or very unlikely to). You can get advice and support from others, but you still have to get there on your own. Therefore start off with what feels good or feels comfortable for you, never mind what everyone else is doing. Think for yourself and follow your own plan and your own goals. Once you have built up a bit of knowledge and experience, you can expand and continue onwards, towards your own 'mountain top', whatever that may be for you.

Katrina Lukies

Article

Kids and Money

by Katrina written in July 2016

Kids and money is such a difficult topic of conversation because every parent has a different view point on how they view money. Especially when it comes to *spending it* on their child/children. For me, the turning point was when my children believed that money came out of those machines in the wall. They thought, as long as you had a plastic card to put in the 'hole in the wall', you could simply get money out. Now that's not incorrect of them to think like that; I liked the idea that children could view money so simply and *believe* that money is always in abundance. If you have that mindset, then that's exactly how it should be. So to me, it was important that my children saw money as freedom, happiness and fun. Not as a means of controlling their lives and limiting their world of possibilities. But like anything; for them to have what they want, they needed to understand a few simple rules first.

Self discipline and work ethic are the first and most important things, and then some basic financial knowledge. Understanding what an investment is, what an asset is and also the power of leverage. We explained to the children that if they found a way of creating or earning money, they could have the ultimate freedom to *spend* it however they like. We come from the point of view that it's *their* money and they don't need our permission to spend it (just like we do as adults). They could also choose to save a certain amount of money and *invest* it, by buying something that *we own*. In return, they would get a regular *rent* payment. So, as an example of this, last year my son Corbyn got himself a pamphlet run which he did twice a week. He would earn an average of $19 per week. I made an agreement with him that if he saved $400, he could buy the '*garage*' off me and I would pay him $10 per week. With his pamphlet run and also a bit of birthday money, he saved $400 within six months. He was now getting $10 a week *plus* still earning an income from his pamphlets. He quickly worked out that he could save another $400 a lot quicker this time as he had two lots of income. He then saved another $400 and bought the '*kitchen*' in our home, which I now also pay him $10 per week for. Now he has $20 a week income from these two assets and was determined to continue this, however I decided he had learned the 'purchasing an asset for income' concept extremely well and now perhaps could think of *other* ways to create more money. This may be in the form of saving some more money and buying an appliance that he can rent to someone, or something similar. Corbyn was able to hand over his pamphlet run a couple of months ago to his older brother Reid, who now wants to do the same thing.

Reid's view on money is more along the lines of "I will save the money towards an investment – *unless* a really good sale comes up on my *steam account"*, or 'the headphones I really want are half price with free shipping so I'm going to buy them now!' So while Reid knows and understands the concept of 'saving to buy an asset', the self discipline to get him to his target of $400 is not as strong as his younger brother's. This *may* show up later in life as having to work longer before he retires, as he lives more day to day and in the moment, rather than going without. It's a bit like when you offer a three year old child a marshmallow. They can have this marshmallow in front of them right now, *or* if they wait for 10 minutes and not eat it, they can have two marshmallows. Most kids will choose to eat the marshmallow they have in front of them, rather than waiting. If they do try and wait out the 10 minutes, they will do everything they can to avoid *looking* at the marshmallow in front of them, or distract themselves so they are not tempted to eat it! It's kind of like this with money too, you can spend your money and have what you want now, or have the discipline to wait for a while and use the money wisely to create *more* money to buy things for the future.

My youngest daughter washes dishes each week for $5 as she is too little to do a pamphlet run yet, but is very keen to takeover in the near future. The hardest part as a parent when your children are saving towards a goal is not to cave in and buy things for them. They need to make their own choices and learn to go without, in order to get what they want. When they leave home as adults and want to save a deposit for their first home or rental property, or even their first car; nobody is going to keep providing them with all the luxuries in life while they save.

So, as our children go forth into this amazing life, they now have the power to make some great decisions regarding their financial wealth. They also know it's not that difficult if they start off with some good money habits; it's just a bit of self discipline, some goals and a plan on how to get there.

MORE RECENT ARTICLES WRITTEN BY GRAEME FOWLER

Article

'Getting Started in Property Investment'

by Graeme Fowler written in 2015.

It's now over 25 years ago that I got started in property investing, and I knew virtually nothing about property – except that I wanted to get rich from it! ☺

I ended up losing about $40,000 on my first property, but luckily I did learn a lot from it.

I made many mistakes along the way and it was really no wonder as I was pretty clueless when it came to all things regarding property investing.

Back then, there wasn't a lot of information around, so it was more of a trial and error thing for me for a few years. There wasn't anyone I knew who I could ask about property investing or get their opinion about something, and virtually nothing written by New Zealander authors on the subject.

I remember a friend of mine inviting me to go see an older guy who apparently was very experienced and successful in investing. It was a year or two after I bought my 1st rental and I still knew almost nothing.

He talked to us about property investing and how prices always double every 7 – 10 years, and it was the best thing you could ever do.

Listening to him, it assured me I had done the right thing as well – by at least *starting* to invest in property.

He also talked to us about commercial property. He had set up a syndicate and was getting 100 people to put in $3,250 each (from memory) into this fund, and we would all own 1% of a commercial building in Wellington. My friend who introduced me had owned an investment property for longer than me and had already bought two of these units in the syndicate, so I decided to buy one as well.

At the time, the guy running this syndicate already had a building in Central Wellington which was available to buy shares in, and this is where our money was invested.

He also showed us a few other properties he was making offers on, and he was going to do the same with lots of properties, as people invested with him.

It all sounded really good, until about five years later when I got a letter to say the company was in liquidation. Several years later I got a cheque in the post and at least got most of the money back that I had put into it.

The guy I looked up to who ran the investments apparently had gone bankrupt.

At the time of hearing the company was in liquidation, it really surprised me. He sounded like he really knew what he was talking about, and was a very wealthy man.

This was a long time ago now, sometime during the 1990's. That was the last I heard of the property investment guru guy that I once looked up to, until a couple of weeks ago when I heard his name in the background on the TV News.

It was to do with a deal he had done in 2008 with his son in law, a very famous All Black. His daughter had married this man which I also had not realised until I heard it on the News.

This guy had bought a property for $900,000 and a few months later, while the GFC and property prices were dropping, sold it to the ex All Black's trust for $1,580,000. A profit of nearly $700,000. The property apparently was only worth around $850,000.

While reading about what happened and further looking into it, the property expert I once thought knew it all, went bankrupt again in 2012.

I don't know why he was bankrupted twice, but it's interesting looking back now as to how naïve I was when I started investing in property. Also, just how many beginning property investors often have no idea where to start, who to talk to, or even why they are getting into it.

I think the biggest thing to ask yourself if you are starting is 'why?'

Is it because it's a popular thing, so it must be good?

Is it because your friends are doing it?

Is it so you can own property for a while and then sell and hopefully *double* your money?

Is it more of a long term goal to have retirement income, or is it just to supplement your other income?

Is it because you dislike your job?

Is it because you love property and have a passion for it?

There are so many reasons that people have, none of which are right or wrong. However your 'why' is essential to know for yourself.

A big enough 'why' or reason for what you're doing will get you through when others may give up, get bored or lose patience.

Or you may have made assumptions such as the guy I looked up to had done, that property prices always double every 7 – 10 years.

Here are some questions a new investor will probably think about, consider, and ask themselves, what is the best thing to do here?

This is after they have a big enough 'why' they want to invest in property.

1. How many properties do I want to own?
2. In what location(s) will they be?
3. Is it best to buy in my city, or outside my city?
4. Should I look to buy properties overseas?
5. What if my city/town is too small and lots of properties are vacant?
6. Is it best to look for areas that have gone up in value more than others, or areas that have had no growth for a long time?
7. Is it best to buy positive cash-flow properties, or negative cash-flow properties?
8. Do I need the properties I buy to go up in value in order to be successful?
9. How much cash-flow do I want from these properties?
10. Do I eventually want to pay off all the mortgages on each property?
11. What is the best option to finance them – Interest Only, P & I, revolving credit or a combination of these?
12. Should I buy new houses as rental properties?
13. Should I buy older character homes for rentals?
14. How do I know what type, construction or age of property is best to buy?

15. How much deposit will I put into each property?
16. Will I ever refinance the property?
17. What is my strategy if prices go up?
18. What is my strategy if prices stay the same?
19. What is my strategy if prices go down?
20. What happens if interest rates go up a few percent, can I still pay the mortgage?
21. Should I join my local Property Investors' Association?
22. Is trading or renovating properties an easy way to make money?
23. Do I need to review my properties regularly?
24. Do I really believe I can be successful?
25. How will I handle things if I make mistakes?
26. What will my family and friends think of me doing this?
27. Does my partner support me in this, or are they against it?
28. What entities or structures should I use - a trust, my own name, a company or something else?
29. What books should I be reading?
30. Do I need to attend any seminars to help me get started?
31. Should I pay for a mentor to help me one on one?
32. How do I know if the mentor is successful or not - or if they just make money from mentoring me, but not from investing themselves?
33. Should I use a property finder to find properties for me?
34. How much time do I have a week I can invest into learning about property and looking at properties to buy?
35. Should I do the maintenance on my properties myself to save money?
36. Will I manage my rentals myself, or use a property manager?
37. How do I know if I'm getting a good tenant and do I need to do a credit check or any other checks?
38. Do I charge a bond and if so how much?
39. How do I know how much to allow for maintenance on my properties each year?

40. Who should I insure my properties with?
41. Do I need malicious damage cover in case the properties get damaged?
42. How much excess should I have on each property for insurance?
43. How does property compare to shares and how do I find out that sort of information?
44. What yield do I want to achieve (annual rent divided by purchase price) when buying my rentals?
45. What is ROI (Return on investment)? And is it important?
46. How do I know what are the best suburbs to invest in?
47. Do I need to avoid any particular streets?
48. What agents and real estate companies should I be talking to?
49. How do I know if the salespeople are telling me the truth or just wanting to sell me a property?
50. How do I get them to call me when they find a suitable property and not other more experienced investors?
51. Should I talk to the banks myself to arrange a loan, or should I use a mortgage broker?
52. Are 1brm, 2brm, 3brm or 4brm properties easiest to rent out to tenants?
53. Should I rent the property by the room or rent to one family like most landlords do?
54. Should I buy apartments or houses?
55. Or should I buy multi-unit blocks?
56. How do I get to know and understand market prices?
57. Do I need to pay for a registered valuation, and how accurate are they?
58. What's the difference between a property's registered valuation, an E-Value, its government valuation (GV, CV or RV) and how does it relate to what the asking price is?
59. Should I buy properties that need work to be done on them or something that needs nothing done?
60. Is it best to buy properties on my own, or in a partnership with someone else?
61. How do I find good tradespeople to deal with?

62. Who is a good accountant I can use that specialises in property investing?
63. How do I find a good lawyer and how much should I be paying?
64. When making offers on properties, how do I know what clauses to use?
65. Do I need to get a LIM report?
66. Should I get a builders report?
67. Do I need to have my finance approved before making any offers?
68. What happens if the banks change *their* rules around lending while I'm still buying?
69. Is there a good time to get into the market?
70. If I wait too long before I start, will I miss all the opportunities?
71. Now, what was my 'why' again?! ☺

These are just some of the questions a beginner may be asking before they are comfortable buying their first rental property.

Some will want all the answers before doing anything, and may never even start. Others like myself started with nothing more than a 'why' I wanted to invest.

There is no right or wrong way to start, and the above questions can be answered in many different ways depending on what you want out of it.

And as you learn more and understand property better over time, there are different *levels* of understanding to the questions above as well.

So far, there have been seven distinct plans or goals I've have gone through over the last 25+ years, and the goals have changed a lot over that time.

Your goals don't have to be set in stone. They can change over time as you get more clarity and know more what it is exactly that you do want. Or when unexpected circumstances occur, like they did with me.

My seven phases so far are as follows:-

i. Get rich in property – that was it! (approx 1989)
ii. Have 10 properties fully paid off by the time I was age 45 with each property giving me about $200 a week after expenses, so approx $100,000 income in total (1994 – 1999)
iii. Own 60 properties, although when I did have 60 properties most were

rent to buys (wraps), or bought as trades and had not yet sold. About 20 were buy and holds at end of 2005 (2000 – 2005)

iv. Not go bankrupt! After an appendix operation and 10 days in hospital, I came out high on drugs and bought about $6 million worth of property in less than two months. The following year I lost over $1.5 million because of it, as well as having $70,000 *negative cash-flow a month* for quite some time. Luckily my foundation was solid, but my property portfolio was reduced down to 40 properties (2006)

v. Consolidate, then starting to rebuild, followed by a separation with a payout settlement to my ex. Now reduced down to 35 properties, 25 of which were buy and holds (2007 – 2011)

vi. Start to slowly rebuild again. Back to 40 properties (2011 – 2013)

vii. Use a new strategy with a new trust and buy 20 properties where the rent had to cover the mortgage, rates, insurance and property management on 20 year P & I loans. Now up to 60 long term buy and holds, 70 properties in total. (2014 - 2015)

This is where I am currently, the goal being to have all mortgages paid off on the 60 rental properties in less than 20 years. The others that were bought as trades are to be sold. Over time, this goal may change as well.

I think 'time' in the property market is more important than 'timing' of the market. Also, at some point you need to make a *start* if you are at all serious about investing.

People tend to fit into two categories when it comes to starting out in property investment:-

1. Those that just get out there and do it. These people learn fast and are not afraid to make mistakes along the way. They know experience will always beat theory. Their downfall is that they can act too soon, buy properties that don't make sense and lose a lot of money quickly.
2. Those that want all their questions answered, and then think of lots more new questions. These people often have been conditioned through the schooling system. They believe it's *bad* to make mistakes. They do everything they can to learn as much as they can, in order not to make a mistake. The fear of making mistakes can prevent them from ever starting to invest, and then come to the conclusion that it's

just too risky.
School teaches us not to make mistakes, but in reality we need to make mistakes and find out for ourselves what works, and what doesn't work. In my book 'NZ Real Estate Investors' Secrets', I interviewed 14 people over the two books, and all the investors do things differently and want different things from investing in property.

Once you do decide to act, you are now taking action and learning as you go. After a while you will then start to gain traction. After you get some traction, eventually it becomes easier for you, and then finally you have attraction. This is where you really get momentum, and it becomes very easy and effortless. At this level, people will come to you and ask you questions, what to do, and how to get started.

It's like a plane taking off on the runway. It moves off very gradually and slowly, it takes a huge amount of energy, noise and effort just to get the plane to move. Then it starts to move slowly along the runway and then starts to develop some speed. Eventually it has enough speed for lift off. It gets off the ground even though it may have a few little wobbles for a while. It is now air-born and flying. Eventually it will get to altitude and be flying almost effortlessly and with great speed. It's only at that point the pilot can ease back, conserve energy and the plane will still fly easily and effortlessly.

In property investing, most people to want to be at altitude *before* they even take off the ground. It doesn't work like that.

My thoughts on the best way to get started are this:-

1. Seriously ask yourself 'why' you want to invest in property. What is *your* big 'why?' A 'why' big enough that will keep you going when things get tough, rules get changed, investors are getting a bad rap in the news, or when you just feel like giving up and selling all your properties.
2. Think about what you want from investing, i.e. how many properties you want to own, how much income from them do you want, and a rough idea of when you want to achieve it by.
3. Read what you can on property investing, talk to a few people that have done it and been successful over at least 15 – 20 years. This can be a minefield too. Investors like me that have been investing for a long time can be stuck in our ways of what works for us. You might talk to

10 successful investors and they all tell you something different, so it can get very confusing.

4. Listen to everyone, and then make your own mind up about what makes sense to you.
5. Have a basic plan and a strategy of how you're going to go about it.
6. Start looking at properties that are for sale that may be suitable for investment.
7. Talk to real estate salespeople, lenders, accountants, lawyers, property managers, and start to build up a good network of people that you can work with over a long time.
8. Rethink your 'why'. Are you really clear before you start investing?
9. Also, are you happy in *all other* areas in your life? If not, you may want to sort those areas first as these distractions can cause you many unseen problems. Whether it's a job you're in that you don't enjoy, your health, poor personal money management, or a relationship that's not working and taking up a lot of your attention. Get these areas working as much as you can before you start.
10. Make a start. At some point you need to put your money on the line and get started.
11. Have fun, celebrate your successes, stay positive and have belief in yourself.

Article

'The Pitfalls and *Stress* of Goal Setting / Planning'

by Graeme Fowler written in 2014.

How many times have you been told you need to set goals and plan for your future? One of the most common methods of goal-setting is the SMART goals – Specific, Measurable, Achievable, Realistic and Time based, i.e. the goals are to be achieved in a certain time-frame. Brian Tracy was another one that had all these specific ways and methods he would teach, that would help people to achieve their goals.

For me, I used to be very focused on goals, working hard to achieve them, and then setting new goals. One overseas seminar I did over 10 years ago was three days just on goal-setting and cost over $10,000 to attend. During the next year or two I did achieve the goals I had set at the time, however I started thinking – 'why wasn't I happy when I achieved a goal, or if I was happy – why was it so short-lived?' The answer I thought was to either set a new and bigger goal or do it in a faster time. I remember being at the course and one of the goals was to own a red Ferrari 355 and also a midnight blue Porsche 911 turbo within the next 12 months. That would make me very happy I thought as I'd always loved fast cars, especially the fast European ones. Within three months I had already bought both of these cars, and while I loved the process of buying them and putting them in my garage at home, something was still missing. 'A Lamborghini' I thought? I always wanted one of them as well, so set a new goal to buy a yellow Lamborghini Murceilago, and another few months later I owned one of them as well. I was very excited at the time, picking it up and driving back to Havelock North. However, although I was happy initially; within a day or so, I was my normal self again and really started to wonder about this whole goal setting *trap*.

It wasn't until maybe a couple of years later that I was listening to an Abraham Hicks CD and it was saying 'you can't arrive happily at your destination by travelling an unhappy journey'. In other words, if you're striving, struggling, working hard to achieve all these goals, there will be no satisfaction at all when you reach them. The answer people think is to set bigger goals, but instead the actual answer is to enjoy the 'now' or the 'process', on the *way* to your goals. Once I understood that, it all started to make sense.

So, in the last few years of 'allowing' goals rather than 'achieving' them, it's almost the opposite of what I used to do, and what most others tend to do.

Think of it in this way: - if you're looking at a stream or a river and you put a canoe in the water, it will naturally go downstream at the speed of the river. If you try to row *upstream* it's very hard work, and unnatural. This is how traditional goal setting very often is. A goal is set, which you think may or may not be achievable; and if it is to be achieved, you will have to work very hard for it. Also a *time* is set by when you want to have the goal achieved by. It's like rowing *upstream* in a river, with the *current* actually *wanting* to take you down-stream. For example, you could say 'my goal is to earn another $100,000 within the next two months by investing in property'. This is an upstream thought (unless you are making that much or more already) and does not make you feel good because there is unnecessary pressure put upon yourself, to achieve it in a given time-frame. On the other hand, if you were to say 'I would like to earn an additional $100,000 and it will come to me in its own good time'. Or 'wouldn't it be nice if I had an extra $100,000 cash in my bank account, and it doesn't have to arrive all once, although it can, and it will come to me in its own time' – these are all *downstream* thoughts. There is no struggle or striving to achieve them, they are very easy, effortless and relaxed.

Just recently I remembered something I had written down along these lines in 2009 which I would read each day for several months, and then totally forgot about it. It went like this: -

The heading was **"Property Trading, Equity in New properties, Renovations"** and then underneath that it said – ***"It would be nice to earn $2 million by using all of these money making streams above. I know it will happen, and it will happen in its own good time. Money flows effortlessly to me in so many different ways, and it is nice to see that every day the $2 million is getting that much closer to me. I'm in full alignment with allowing the $2 million to come to me in its own time, in its own way, and through all the various ways that money flows to me. Every day I enjoy what I'm doing, I love what I'm doing, and this too helps me get closer and closer to allowing all of the $2 million to come to me".***

I realised a couple of months ago that just in this year (2014) what I was doing with a new property investing strategy, it was already done!

It's almost like having a 'knowing' that it's already done when you put it out there – what you actually want, and then drop it, or carry on with life. Another way of saying it is this – if you're watching say the All Blacks play Australia live in a rugby test match and it's a close game, there will be highs and lows during the 80 minutes of the game. You may not know the actual result of who wins until the full 80 minutes is up, so it can be very tense watching the game. But if you knew the result and were watching it on *replay*, now the emotions, the worry, the frustrations don't come into it - as you *know* how it all ends up. It's the same with goals, having the knowing that it will all work out well in the end. You don't worry when things that don't work out as you think they should along the way, because you *know* how it ends. Watching a movie for the 2nd or 3rd time is the same, you don't have all the highs and lows wondering how it all turns out, because you know how it *finishes*. That is how you want to look at goals, *allowing* them rather than *striving*, or working hard for them.

So, rather than forcing yourself to go look at properties because you think you *need to* do this in order to achieve your goals, do it only when you feel the *inspiration* to do so. Not because you think you have to, or because you may fail and look bad to others if you don't do it. People often say procrastination is a bad thing, but I don't think it is bad at all. If you are not inspired to get off the couch and go look at properties, or go to the bank to ask for finance etc, then just wait until you *have* the inspiration to do so. It will be a far more enjoyable process. The answer is to have a happy journey on the *way* to what you want, and enjoying the process. Then when you get there, you will also be happy with the end result/goal. The other important thing too is, over time your goals may change to something else. Some goals you may either decide not to do at all, or not go for what you originally had intended. By enjoying the process on the way, you will be a lot happier - no matter what the eventual outcome is.

This is about as specific as I would get now on setting any goals:

Write down this about what you want:-

*When – 0% (achieved by when)

*What – 8% (specifics of income, number of properties, cash-flow etc)

*How – 2% (how you are going to do it)

*Why – 90% (why you want it?)

I have rated above what I think the *importance* of each of these four things is, as a percentage.

As you can see I don't rate a time (the When) to achieve goals as of any importance at all, the 'How' is also very low in importance. The 'What' you want is more important, but the most important in all of this is your 'Why'. Without a big enough 'Why', the chances of getting what you want are very slim. This is another big key to it all, and without a big 'Why' you will find excuses and reasons along the way that will keep you exactly where you are.

For me, my big 'Why' back when I started investing was that I didn't want to work for someone for 40 years or more, and end up with nothing at age 65.

I wanted to learn about finance and investing so that I didn't end up broke at the end of my life. Also the freedom to do what I wanted to, and go on holiday when I felt like it was a big part of my 'Why' as well. And not having to answer to a boss or ask permission to take time off, with only a few weeks holiday each year.

One last thing when it comes to goal setting/investing – *good investing* is <u>supposed</u> to be boring! I love looking for properties to buy and I especially like the negotiation side of things, it's exciting. However once a property is financed and tenanted, it will just sit there and pretty much do nothing for the next 20 years or so, slowly getting paid off. After it's purchased not a lot really happens, so it *seems* boring. That's how it's *supposed* to be.

If you want more excitement in your life, look for it in other areas. Do the things you love to do that give you that excitement. But keep your investing safe. When people try to make *investing* their excitement, they will make silly decisions and eventually end up costing themselves a lot of money. People will often gamble or buy lotto tickets for the excitement of it, for the thrill of possibly winning. Don't do that with your investing, keep your investing safe and keep it boring.

Remember *good investing* is boring ☺

Article

'Building a Foundation/ Cash-flow'

by Katrina Lukies written in Dec 2015

I often get asked the question 'have you bought any houses lately' and my response is 'no - I'm not buying at the moment. I'm waiting for the cash-flow on my existing properties to balance out'.

When I started my investment portfolio, the first thing I got clear on was my plan. Over the next three years I wanted to buy ten investment properties at around 10 - 12% yield. They would need to break even on 20 year P&I loans, including rates, insurance and property management fees, a fairly basic plan overall.

I was very fortunate living with Graeme to see how easy it can be to buy houses, and so being armed with my mentor I was away. 2014/15 was a booming market in Flaxmere and within a year I had already purchased six properties following my criteria above. Shoot before long I will be retired and living the dream I thought!

But when I took a step back I noticed something that didn't feel right to me, it was cash-flow. Why was my revolving credit increasing month by month? Surely it should be around the same each month, if not slightly decreasing I thought. I had bought well and most of my properties were actually cash-flow positive. Time to investigate further!

The two main reasons were actually vacant houses and repairs/maintenance costs. Both of these are unavoidable expenses that may seem fairly small at the time, but when combined, they can turn your cash-flow around quickly. A heat pump, insulation and a new hot water cylinder for one property, at the same time tenants giving notice in another house that needed painting, carpets and curtains before I could rent it out again. Also, already having a vacant property meant cash-flow was hugely negative. Better keep the day job for a bit longer I thought.

My revolving credit had taken a big hit, and for me it didn't feel comfortable to continue buying houses whilst my already existing portfolio wasn't holding its own for now.
Graeme was continuing to get amazing deals and selling them to other

investors, and these were properties that I really wanted. Excellent yields, high rents, good areas, 3 bedroom homes with garages, and unbelievable bargain prices. Everyone was experiencing the rising house prices in Flaxmere and the houses were selling extremely fast. Maybe a good plan would be to finish off buying the last four properties before the house prices get too high, and I can't get my yields!! Then I could just revalue them and borrow more money, after all interest rates are amazingly low, house prices are increasing, and I have a good job with steady income.

But ....

This means I would need to get my existing houses revalued costing me more money. My LVR would be right on its limit (80%) and personally it didn't feel comfortable for me, any slight movement in the banks position or the market meant I could lose it all. I reviewed my plan and realised I was already ahead of my target by at least a year, so I decided to wait for a least six months to see what the cash-flow with the existing properties is like after that.

With it being nearly Christmas, I decided to review my position again and this time I realised some things needed to change. Graeme casually mentioned that the tenants in one of my properties were behind in rent and another lot had given notice! With that I threw my toys out of the sandpit, had a small hissy fit, cursed property investing and generally felt shitty.

A few days later upon reflection of my situation, Graeme offered to look over my bank statements to see what's going on. Handing me his iPad to pull up my internet banking, I had five minutes of silence while he scrolled up and down asking the odd questions here and there. Questions like 'what did you buy at shoe clinic?' or 'why is there Subway on here?' I of course had perfectly valid answers to all his questions!

Overall he concluded that the situation wasn't really that bad, and the only real reason that the revolving credit was going more into debt was from the maintenance on the properties. But on the positive side, the properties were increasing in value with the much needed work being done on them. So I asked Graeme one of his favourite questions 'what would you do in my situation?'

So here is my 2016/17 plan. I plan to put $1,000 month into the trust via wages and other investments over the next two years, as well as fixing a large portion of the revolving credit into a 15 year loan. This will take advantage of the low interest rates. Being able to fix on a lower interest rate than the floating rate, thus saving me money over the long term. Currently, because I have bought well and not revalued the properties, my LVR is at 70% and will continue to improve as I pay down the mortgages.

This means in no time at all, with a few good money habits and a bit of patience I will be in a strong position to buy more houses, having a good solid foundation regardless of what the market is doing.

A solid foundation to a beginner investor like me means 65-70% LVR, ability for properties to break even, good cash-flow from other sources to provide for maintenance/repairs or even new legislation, and good money habits to reduce the revolving credit.

It does mean my personal spending like holidays is restricted, a few less meals out and yes I have to continue working (for now) but it allows me to safely build my investment portfolio, and await the benefits in the near future.

Article

'Building a Solid Foundation in Real Estate'

by Graeme Fowler written in 2011.

With a large number of well known property investors in NZ going bankrupt, soon after the GFC in 2008, this may be a good time to take a look at your own property portfolio or investment strategies. Many of these investors were also promoters and charged thousands of dollars (at times tens of thousands) to mentor the unwary or naive beginning investor, and often charged for their investing seminars and related materials. If they were so successful and could teach others how to invest and some even tell investors which way the market was going to go (up or down and by how much!) by using various indicators, why have most of these so called experts gone bankrupt themselves - or very close to it? A few of them in my opinion were always out for themselves. In other words deliberately sold or promoted dodgy investments, or had strategies which were just never going to work. Even though a few of us warned other investors about several of these so called and self professed property gurus, they still had a lot of followers that went along with everything they said, as if they were some sort of Messiah or similar. They could do no wrong in their eyes and believed every word they said. Surely you would think with the amount they charged for their mentoring services, seminars, subscriptions, blogs and other products and materials, they would have huge sums of money to invest with, and invest it wisely, i.e. with low risk strategies. You would think they would still be very well off today.

I believe it's because none of them had built a solid foundation to begin with. When you build a home, the most important part, and the part that takes the longest to build, is the foundation. In property investing, one of the attributes that goes into building a good *solid* foundation, is buying rental properties that the average family will want to rent. For example, a 2, 3 or 4brm home, in a reasonable location and in tidy order.

Other not so obvious building blocks for your solid foundation include putting down a 20% deposit on each property you buy (as opposed to borrowing against equity gained on any other properties owned), having sufficient cash-flow to cover all your expenses with each property, preferably a 20 year or *less* P & I loan (25 year loan possibly if the cash-flow is tight, but never 30 years), and buying below market value by knowing your market well. Following this you will build equity each year in your property portfolio (that is with a static or rising market. On a market where property prices drop over the year, it will depend on how much you pay off principal compared to the drop in property prices whether you build any equity or not).

If you use the interest only approach as so many investors still do, and the method usually taught by the promoters mentioned above, amongst many others, you are only building equity when the property market is *rising*. You lose equity when the property prices are going down. Out of all the hundreds and hundreds of investors that I've met, less than a handful have used the 'interest only' strategy well. Each of these investors have sufficient cash-flow from elsewhere (other property strategies or a business etc), a low LVR ratio, or they specialise in commercial type multi-unit properties often worth in the millions of dollars to purchase. For the average investor using I/O, I do not know of anyone trying to build a good solid property portfolio (apart from these few people) that I would say has a good, rock solid foundation. There may be a few people out there, but I have never met them.

This is what I would class as a good solid foundation in which to build from: -

1) Using P & I loans –

(i) never borrow more than 80% of the purchase price (not the property value) when buying

(ii) take out a loan of 25 years and preferably less

(iii) buy the next investment property *only* when another 20% is saved (not from refinancing existing properties)

(iv) cash-flow to cover all the outgoings - including rates and insurance.

By doing this, I believe by the time you have 8 – 10 properties, you will have a good sound foundation on which to build from. I would not borrow against any increased equity at any stage to buy further rental properties - even if they have doubled in value, or your borrowing is below 50% on any of the properties.

2) Using Interest only loans –

(i) never borrow more than 70% of the purchase price (not the property value) when buying

(ii) purchasing the next property only when another 30% is saved (not from refinancing existing rentals as mentioned above)

(iii) cash-flow to cover all the outgoings - including rates and insurance.

I would also add that until you get to a level where your portfolio (using I/O) reaches 20 - 25 rental properties, a debt level of 60% or less (by paying off more debt when you are able to) and a positive cash-flow after all expenses of a minimum of $5,000 per month, you haven't got a good foundation. Anything less than this using I/O is in my opinion a time bomb waiting to go off, and any unforeseen circumstances that come along could wipe out everything you've worked for. It's just way too risky, and not worth gambling everything on.

You may have heard the difference between *good debt* and *bad debt* and to a certain point I agree with what others say about this. It is very beneficial to use good debt (debt that somebody else pays you to own) to help you leverage your money while you are in the building stage of your property portfolio. However there comes a time when you will hopefully say to yourself – "this is a level I'm comfortable with, and now rather than buying any more properties, I will focus more on directing any excess money into paying down debt on my rental properties at a faster rate than what I have been doing". Paying *all* of your debt off, therefore being totally debt free is what the ultimate goal (in my opinion) should be.

In my property portfolio, I have 9 existing loans at the moment (out of 40 properties) with loans of less than $65,000 on each, one of them being a mortgage of only $38,000 on a property with a market value of approx $200,000.

Assumptions

If you have the assumption that property prices consistently go up in value over time, that very thought could cost you everything you want to achieve with your real estate investing (more so if you use interest only).

Here are a few other assumptions that have caught people out in the last few years.

1. I'm good at buying properties below market price - *therefore* I am a good investor
2. I am good investor, therefore I am *also* a good property trader

3. I am good at business and have made lots of money by running a successful business, therefore I will *also* be good at real estate investing
4. I am a good property investor, therefore I am *also* good at speculating with design and builds, buying sections and sub-dividing properties
5. That person is well known and speaks so smoothly and with confidence on stage, I will be able to learn a lot from him/her
6. The person speaking on stage is very enthusiastic about what they are selling. It must be amazing what they are selling, plus so many other people agree with what he's saying. It has to be genuine
7. I would never buy outside Wellington, Auckland or Christchurch - the smaller towns just don't have any capital gains {(i)if you *rely* on <u>any</u> capital gains, to me you are not an investor but more of a speculator, (ii) over the last 50 years or so in NZ, cities with 100,000 or more population have had an average *percentage per annum* growth rate within approx 1%, compared to the other cities in NZ)}
   N.B. Please see 'What's the Real Estate Market Doing!!!!!?????' article on Page 117
8. This person has written a book on property investing, I will follow their plan and therefore will also be successful
9. This person knows exactly which locations will go up in value as opposed to other areas, I will therefore follow their advice on where to buy and when to sell
10. I've heard that tax liens are the way to go, there is so much money to be made with them. I'm going over to the U.S. to investigate further and then invest for myself
11. These people on this property chat forum have written well over 1,000 posts telling other investors how to do it, they *must* know what they're talking about (for every one of these posters on property forums that does know something about investing, another four or five know very little about it, and often spoil it for the new people wanting to learn)
12. Property is the best investment you can ever make, you will never lose money by investing in property

So these are some of the assumptions that people have made about property investing – more so in the last 10 years or so. When you assume anything like what is mentioned above, you stop thinking for yourself. When you stop thinking for yourself and follow others blindly, you are not taking responsibility and you also have an excuse to blame others if things go wrong for you. In other words – it's not your fault. So take responsibility, don't follow the crowd, think for yourself, and if something sounds too good to be true - 99% of the time it is.

For me, I've had two major threats to my property investment portfolio, and without a good solid foundation when these events happened, either one of them would have wiped me out as well.

The most recent (12 months ago) was a separation with my partner of 16 years which cost me a lot of money and is something I would not want to go through again!

The other threat or event that happened was about six years ago. It's a long story which was written about in my updated book in 2008 ("NZ Real Estate Investors' Secrets"), with me losing approx $1.5 million over the 12 months from the end of 2005 to the end of 2006. It all stemmed from me being in hospital with peritonitis (burst appendix) and coming out of hospital 10 days later on such a high with all the drugs, etc. I bought about $6 million worth of property and cars over the following two months, breaking most of my own investing rules - and it nearly cost me everything. For a long time my cash-flow was approx $70,000 a month *negative*. So going backwards by $70,000 each and every month, selling these properties and cars I had just bought at huge discounts, as well as selling around 20 properties from my existing rental portfolio (I had about 65 properties at the time) was the only way I could save it all. But without the solid foundation that I'd built up over the previous years, I would have been left bankrupt, like a lot of other investors have ended up today.

So in summary, take a look at your own property portfolio, or if you are just beginning - look at various potential threats or dangers and create a plan that is as safe as you can possibly make it. Build a solid foundation, there is no rush. Build it solid enough so that it can withstand any potential threats you think could happen one day. A lot of the time we have assumptions, not realising they are just assumptions, and are not based on any facts. Read books, talk to other successful people that also invest, but always think for yourself.

Have fun along the way and celebrate your successes, safe investing.

Article

'Building a Solid Foundation in Real Estate' Part 2,

by Graeme Fowler written in 2015.

The first article I wrote four years ago on building a foundation was an outline of why it's so important. Especially if you're serious about investing and want it to be one of, if not your main source of wealth and income long term. If property investing is more of a hobby than a passion, then it's not so important.

So if you want to be more actively involved and reliant on property investing for an income in the future; here are some things that will make your overall foundation *stronger,* and also some things that will make your foundation *weaker.*

All these will make it stronger.

1. Buying any property below market value
2. Paying a deposit of at least 20% - 30% when purchasing
3. Not refinancing existing properties at any time
4. Increase in market prices of your properties (outside your control)
5. Having good tenants, and or property managers
6. Keeping up with any maintenance that needs doing
7. Using P & I loans to gradually pay down your mortgages
8. If loans are fixed at a higher interest rate than current rates, pay down up to 5% p.a. on the outstanding balance, on as many loans as you can
9. Increase your equity in your portfolio every year (reducing LVR)
10. Buying more properties and repeating the above

All these will make it weaker.

1. Paying market price or above (not knowing market prices well enough)
2. Putting in low or no deposits when buying properties
3. Using high registered valuations and then refinancing, or refinancing if prices go up. In other words – revaluing your portfolio and borrowing

on increased equity

4. Property prices falling
5. Using interest only loans
6. Not doing maintenance on properties when it's required, and so you end up getting lower rents
7. Not reducing your LVR every year
8. Selling properties because you think they are not performing (going up in value)
9. Increasing debt with every purchase. I.e. your LVR may stay the same, but when buying new properties, the overall amount of debt always increases
10. Buying more properties and repeating the above

Many people come to me or e-mail me, having already been doing a lot of the things mentioned above. All the things that make their foundation weaker, not stronger. As time goes by, more and more properties are purchased and then refinanced (people will also often do this on their own homes).

Then they are often refinanced again to a high debt level if prices go up. This is usually using unrealistic registered valuations, which aren't worth the paper they are written on.

Now instead of building a strong and solid foundation, they are in fact building a *negative* foundation. It would look kind of like an *upside* down pyramid. A foundation that gets easier and easier to fall over and be destroyed with any unexpected circumstances that can arrive at any time. Things such as a change in tax or government policy, loss of income from a job, a separation, interest rate increases, changes in LVR rules, property prices falling etc.

Lots of investors lost everything who were investing in Auckland around 2007 – 2008 with only a 5% or so decrease in prices. If their foundation was strong to begin with, this would not have happened.

The safest of all ways, and to have the most solid foundation in property investing would be to have *no debt* at all. To me that is the end goal, i.e. when you feel you have enough income from your properties, and are not buying any more to hold long term; start focusing on paying off *all* the debt.

That way if interest rates went up very high, or market prices say halved in value, then it would have no affect on you.

That's not practical when you're starting out, so you do want to use leverage, but use it *responsibly.*

By using it responsibly, this would be (as mentioned above) using a 20 – 30% deposit on properties purchased, and not refinancing them. By doing this, you are using a small portion of your own money and borrowing a larger part from the bank to buy properties. This is called leverage - or doing 'more with less'.

With any form of leverage there are risks associated.

In the case of buying properties with a small deposit, the main risks are:-

1. The banks want their money back at short notice
2. Interest rates increase to a point where you are having to top up the mortgages yourself
3. Prices decrease and you lose your equity

The other leverage which you are using with P & I loans is the leverage of *other* peoples' time and money. This to me is what a true 'investment' is – i.e. something that somebody else *pays you* to own.

With P & I loans, the rent received goes towards your mortgage and slowly pays the loan off that you have with your bank.

At the start of the loan, you are paying almost all interest and very little principal. As time goes on, you pay more and more principal and less and less interest.

To start with, it seems almost pointless paying off such a little amount of principal, and you may think why even bother?

But by using this method (as opposed to interest only where *nobody* is paying off the loan) you do start to see results, and even more so if you have several properties.

It may be that you only pay $200 - $300 a month off the principal part of the loan early on, but if you had 10 properties like this, it would be $2,000 - $3,000 a month.

This increases slightly each and every month as I mentioned, until at the end of the loans you will be paying almost *no* interest, and almost *all* principal.

For me at the moment, about $6,250 a week or $27,000 a month gets paid off principal. That's over $300,000 a year and this will keep increasing until all the loans are paid off in full (however as each loan get paid back in full, this amount of principal getting paid off each month *drops* until you redirect the extra cash-flow you get now, into paying down another loan faster). If market prices of my properties go up, go down or stay the same, it doesn't matter at all because it's not only *not important*, but irrelevant to my overall picture or plan.

You may have heard of the example of taking 1c at the start of the month and doubling it every day for one month (31 days) and being surprised at how much it grows to.

At day one, it would be 1c, day two it will be 2 cents, day three 4 cents and so on.

After 10 days, it's still only $5.12 which is about 1/3 of the way through the month.

Day 15 is $164, so still not a lot considering its already *half* way through the month.

At day 20 it would have grown to just over $5,000 and so looking a bit healthier.

Day 25 it's now $168,000, day 26 is $335,000, day 27 is $671,000 and at day 28 finally a million dollars is reached with $1.34 million.

Then another three days later at day 31 being the end of the month, it has now grown to an amazing $10,737,000!

That is the power of compounding.

When you use the power of leverage combined with the power of compounding; you can achieve what seemed like the impossible, in a relatively short period of time.

Doing this sensibly in a way that you strengthen your foundation with each and every property purchase with leverage and the power of compounding, you will be well on your way to achieving great financial success.

Article

'How To Have More Luck In Property Investing'

by Graeme Fowler written in 2014.

People will often say to me, you were lucky that you got in at a good time when you started your investing, you couldn't do that now. Or, it was lucky you found some good agents to help you find properties when you started, there's too much competition from other investors now.

Roger Hamilton uses a word analogy with the word 'Luck', mostly with operating a business and comparing it to a game of soccer (football).

I've used it below in a similar way to show you how it works if you are a property investor, and want to become luckier!

Location.

In the game of football, you may think someone like Christian Ronaldo or Lionel Messi is lucky in the way the ball is passed to them, and all they have to do is kick it past the goal keeper to get a goal. And they get paid millions of dollars each year to do that. You might think, well I could kick the ball past them too, it looks so easy – why not me?

The first letter stands for location which means being in the right place at the right time.

The same applies in real estate – where are you *located* when all the deals are happening? Are you out working in a job or a business, or are you doing work around your properties because you think you're saving money?

So location is very important. You need to be in a location and available to act quickly when you need to.

Understanding.

With football, the players must understand *why* they are there. What is their purpose, or intention for being in the right location? They need to understand that their purpose is to get as many goals as they can.

In real estate, you also need to have an understanding of what you want to achieve. What are your financial goals, what plan are you following and what are your rules for investment? You need to have a good understanding of what you are doing, and why you are doing it.

Connections.

You can be standing in the right place and also understand why you are there in the game of soccer; but you might turn around and nobody is there, or wonder why nobody is passing you the ball. That is where connections are very important. You need to have a good team of people around you that will pass you the ball so that you can score the goals.

You must have good connections in real estate investing too, a good team of people you can rely on in many areas. These people will let you know about any potential deals, whether it's real estate salespeople or other investors passing you deals. You may also have various tradespeople available to do maintenance on your properties that need doing from time to time. This would include plumbers, builders, painters, electricians, carpet/lino layers etc. If you don't manage your own properties, you will need to have good property managers to find you tenants, do inspections, and make sure the rent gets paid on time. You will also have people who handle the legal side of things for you when buying and selling properties, also an accountant to do your accounts at the end of each financial year.

All of these are very important people who you will form part of your team, or your *connections*.

Knowledge.

This is where you must know the rules of the game. In soccer you must know what you can and can't do to stay on the field of play. You must have an in-depth knowledge of the game itself.

In real estate, you must also have knowledge in many areas.

Firstly, the city you are investing in. What streets should you avoid buying in, are there any suburbs you should stay away from?

You'll also need to know what the market value of properties are in your area, properties that are similar to ones you want to buy. If you don't have an in-depth knowledge of the market, how will you know if you are getting a good deal or not?

Do you know how to negotiate well both as a buyer and a seller?

How do you structure your offers when buying property, what do you do if you are bidding at an auction? There are other things you should be knowledgeable about as well. Things like what are your banks' lending criteria, what yield do you need from your rental properties when buying, what are the current bank interest rates for borrowing, how to keep good records for your accountant, what it will cost if you need to do maintenance or renovations on a property when buying, all sorts of things you will need to have good *knowledge* of.

You.

You may have all of the above and yet still not succeed. In the game of football, if nobody on your team likes or respects you, they may not even want you to score any goals, so will keep the ball to themselves.

You will need to be a good team player and know that most of the time – you need them more than they need you. Investing in real estate can be the same, how do other people see you?

Do you have a good reputation in the eyes of these people?

Why should they do business with you?

Your reputation and integrity are very important, and can be the make or break of your success.

When you say you're going to do something, do you do it? Or do you have a reason or excuse why you didn't follow through? Some people think – saying you're going to do something, then not doing it, plus a good excuse - is the same as actually doing it.

You need to be able to relate to others, and they relate to you.

Are you approachable when people ask something of you, or do you not have any time for anybody apart from yourself?

Do you get easily distracted from your goals or your plan?

Can you stick within your rules for investing, or break them because things seem boring to you?

Will you keep going when the going gets tough and it would be so much easier to quit?

Do you have good money management skills?

Can you oversee your entire operation to make sure everything is operating and performing as it should be?

Think of yourself as a stock on the share-market.

Would other people invest in you if you were a stock they could buy?

Would they see value in you, and see the long term prospects?

Or would they want to buy now and then sell again in a short space of time because they see too much long term risk in *you*?

All of these are important things to look at for yourself.

If you look at each of these – 'Location', 'Understanding', 'Connections', 'Knowledge' and 'You', the 'You' is the most important, and brings it all together.

You could be perfect in all other areas and get this wrong – and it could cost you everything you've worked for. So it's important to make sure you're someone that people want to do business with, and can relate to.

If you take a look at each of these five things in detail, then rate yourself honestly from 1 to 10 in each.

You may give yourself a low rating in some and a high rating in others. By doing this, you will immediately see what you need to do in order to improve your *own* rating in each area.

When you can honestly say to yourself that you are 9 or above in *each* of the L.U.C.K.Y. areas, then you will find that you do indeed become luckier in the eyes of not only others, but yourself as well.

However *luck* really had nothing to do with it at all ☺

Article

‘What Does Cash-flow Positive Mean?’

by Graeme Fowler written in 2015.

I will often ask at seminars or meeting up with other investors – what are some of your rules for investing?

Most will say that one of their rules is to ‘only buy cash-flow positive properties’.

I will say – ‘well, what does that mean?’

They will often look at me as if to think I’ve never heard of the saying ‘cash-flow positive’ before. So, they say ‘well it has to make money!’

I say – ‘ok so let’s say I buy a house for $200,000 with no mortgage and it rents for $100 a week, is that cash-flow positive?’

They say ‘no it’s not’.

And I say ‘well it actually *is!*’

It is according to some people - it just depends on what your definition of cash-flow positive is.

Here are the things that are taken into consideration in order to work out if a property is cash-flow positive, or not.

First of all, you have the *rent* which is a fixed amount per year. Some people, when working out if something is cash-flow positive or not, will use 52 weeks rent for the year, others will use 50 weeks of the year and some will use 48 weeks. Using 48 weeks or 50 weeks takes into account any vacancies or loss of rent. I always use 52 weeks.

Then comes the interesting part, as there are so many variables that people use to work it out.

Here is a list of factors/expenses which can be used to work out if something is cash-flow positive or not:-

Council Rates

Regional Rates

Water Rates

Insurance

Property Management

Maintenance

And after that, you also have the interest rate per annum of the loan, the term of the loan (how many years the loan is to be paid off over), the amount of deposit used when purchasing the property, and finally, whether you're using a P & I loan, or an interest only loan.

Simply saying something is cash-flow positive or not really is meaningless, without knowing how they are calculating it.

With the example above, some would call that positive cash-flow, which of course it is if you are using a certain *method* of determining it.

From the above you can see that there are so many different ways of working out if a property is cash-flow positive or not, so here are some of the main ones people use.

N.B. None of them are right or wrong, and with no mortgage or a low mortgage on a property as mentioned above, you can pretty much call any property cash-flow positive if it's rented.

Rent (anywhere from 48 to 52 weeks) per annum - must be more than expenses (to be considered cash-flow positive).

Method 1: - Loan on interest only (I/O). No deposit when purchasing the property, and using all of the expenses above (some investors don't include the maintenance part in their calculations).

Lots of investors manage their properties themselves, and therefore don't have 'property management' to consider in their calculations.

Method 2: - As above, but the loan is on Principal and Interest (P & I). What does have a huge effect on this is how long the *term* of the loan is over. If the loan was over only 10 years for example, it would be very difficult if not impossible to have the property be cash-flow positive, as the *repayments* on the loan would be so much higher than they would be on a 20 or 25 year loan.

Method 3: - Loan on interest only. Use a 20% deposit when purchasing each property and using the expenses above as required.

Method 4:- As above using a 20% deposit and using P & I over a specific term, usually 20 or 25 years, and some people even use 30 years.

I've used two different methods to work out if the properties I was buying were cash-flow positive, or at least neutral (rent is approx equal to calculated expenses).

The first method was when I was buying rentals about 12 – 14 years ago and building up a good solid foundation. What I wanted then was to have the rent cover my expenses on either a 20 or 25 year loan, while using a 20% deposit for each purchase.

The deposit was created/made, or saved each time by either trading properties, or renovating properties and selling them on again. Other investors may save this deposit from their wages, or save it from the cash-flow from owning a good business. In the early 2000's interest rates were a lot higher than they are now, around 8 – 10% per annum compared to around 4.5% p.a. now, so it was a lot more difficult to get a property to be cash-flow positive, or even neutral back then. That is, unless you used interest only, or put in a reasonable deposit when buying any rental properties.

The other method I used was early last year when I set up a new trust to purchase 20 rental properties. These properties were to be purchased with no deposit and they had to be at least cash-flow neutral or slightly positive, using a 6.5% p.a. interest rate as a guide. This was over the *entire* 20 properties, so occasionally one property may be slightly negative, but the other ones being cash-flow positive would have to make up for this.

The expenses that the rent had to cover - was the mortgage, rates, regional rates, insurance and also property management on a 20 year P & I loan.

I didn't factor in an amount for maintenance, however over the last two years this has worked out at approximately $1,000 - $1,200 a month over the entire 20 properties ($50 - $60 for each property).

With these 20 properties that I bought last year, the income after expenses (rates, insurance & property management) is approx $18,500 a month and the mortgage amount is approx $17,000 a month.

Most of these loans are still fixed at 5.75% - 6% p.a. and if they come down to around 4.5% p.a. (current interest rates) when the fixed terms expire during next year, the mortgage payments will then drop down to about $15,500 a month.

That would make them $3,000 a month cash-flow positive ($150 per property) which is more than enough to cover any maintenance.

So, there are many, many ways of determining if something is cash-flow positive or not: -

1. Various methods of using *some* or *all* of the expenses, and some investors may even calculate this by using none of the expenses.
2. Also whether you are using I/O or P & I loans. If using P & I loans, what term is the loan over? Is it over 10 years, 15 years, 20 years, 25 years or 30 years?
3. And how much deposit is paid when purchasing each property? Is it on no deposit (100% financed) or is it with a 5%, 10%, 20%, 30%, 40% or even more deposit?

You may understand now why it can get very confusing for people at times, or hearing other investors talk about their investing rules, and wanting only to buy *cash-flow positive* properties. ☺

Article

'What could You do with $60,000 Cash?'

by Graeme Fowler written 2015

This question was asked to five of us for the NZ Property Investors' magazine for an article. Below is my answer to it, however it was only supposed to be 400 words for the magazine, so here it is in full:-

With $60,000 in cash, there's quite a lot you could do without too much risk. However it does depend a lot though on your strategy, your plan, your own financial intelligence, and how risky *you* are as an investor.

Lots of people use risky strategies that will most likely cost them everything in the long run. They try to pick which area to invest in; in other words, what locations they think will go up in value. They invest with assumptions, hopes and wishful thinking, not with logic and common sense.

It doesn't even come into my thinking as to what I think will happen with prices, as it has no relevance to me. It only has any relevance if you want, expect, or hope that prices will go up, i.e. strategies that *rely* on that happening for your plan to work.

I don't ever know what's going to happen, and neither does anybody else know. Also I don't care if property prices go up, down or stay the same for the next 20 years. My strategy and plan will work in all markets.

Last year I bought 20 rentals effectively using no money, and they were still cash-flow positive on 20 year P & I mortgages. So with $60,000 cash there are safe options to use, *if* you have the experience.

What I would do is look for properties that were suitable as rentals, with yields of 9% – 10% or so in locations such as Hawkes Bay, possibly Rotorua, Wainuiomata and maybe Feilding. I know you can get good quality, good location and easy to rent properties in Hawkes Bay with those yields, and I'm pretty sure with some looking around I could find them in those other areas as well. I would rule out a lot of the bigger cities where the yields are way too low. It doesn't make sense to buy there and the only reason people do accept such minimal yields, is they think that prices will keep going up. That may or may not happen, but personally I never base investing decisions on what could be. To do so would be very risky, plus you would most likely have to top up the mortgages as well.

ARTICLE 'WHAT COULD YOU DO WITH $60,000 CASH?'

Knowing Hawkes Bay so well, I would look for something I could buy below market value and either add value to it, or rent as it is. For example, let's say a property was worth $170,000 and I bought it for $150,000. I would initially borrow $120,000 (80% of the purchase price). This would use half of the $60,000 cash ($150,000 - $120,000 = $30,000). This property would easily rent for $300p.w. and the mortgage on a 20 year P & I loan would be about $180 a week. Rates, insurance and property management would be another $70 a week or so, leaving it cash-flow positive by $50 a week (not including any maintenance).

So, you could use the other $30,000 to do the same and you would have two properties being paid off in full by the tenants in 20 years. You would have a cash-flow of about $100 a week, which should comfortably cover any maintenance.

What I would do though, is look for another one asap and do the same. And, because I had bought the first one so well, I would look to refinance it as quickly as possible, to give me back as *much* of the initial deposit as I could. In this case, let's say the first property valued up to $170,000. After three to six months, the bank should allow you (or immediately after any renovations etc) to refinance your original loan, providing you get a registered valuation from a valuer that the bank has on their approved list. If it values to say $170,000 the bank will let you borrow 80% of that - which is now $136,000. This would cost another $20 or so a week in mortgage payments, but you would still be cash-flow positive. You have now used effectively only $14,000 of your original $60,000 ($30,000 minus the $16,000 given back by refinancing: $136,000 - $120,000).

Using this with the same figures you could buy four properties (4 x $14,000 = $56,000). You will now see by buying even better, or having the valuation work more in your favour (valuations can vary hugely) you may need a lot less equity per property than even this. I would be looking to buy at 20% below what I know I could get them to value to, which would mean I'm not using any of the $60,000 cash at all, after they are refinanced. You need to allow some money for maintenance though, so I think you could comfortably buy 10 properties this way (end result of $6,000 equity used per property) and be okay.

With the 20 properties I bought last year, so far the maintenance on these works out to be an average of about $1,000 a month total over the 20 properties. To show how it would look using $6,000 equity each time, it would be something like this: -

Purchase price $145,000.

Initial deposit (20%) $29,000.

Revalue several months later to $174,000.

Bank will lend 80% of that which is $139,000.

In effect, $6,000 equity used ($145,000 - $139,000).

One important thing to me is if you do refinance like this, don't *ever* refinance them again after that! Let them just sit there with all the mortgages reducing over time until all of them are paid off in full. A common mistake a lot of people make is refinancing their investment properties (and often their own home) when the market goes up. They use the extra equity to buy more properties, sometimes refinancing several times and never bringing their LVR down. This is a recipe for disaster which has already cost hundreds of investors in New Zealand everything they've worked for and built up, thinking the market always goes up. It doesn't ☺

So in summary, let's say I ended up buying the 10 rental properties using $6,000 equity for each, and they all had a market value of say $150,000. That would be $1.5 million (10 x $150,000 properties) worth of property purchased using the initial $60,000 of equity. The tenants will have paid off all the mortgages after 20 years.

At that stage any upward movement in prices would have been a bonus if you did want to sell any of the properties; otherwise you would have around $10,000 a month in rent after all expenses coming in from 10 debt free rental properties.

Another way to look at it is this; the original $60,000 cash has been used as leverage using other people's money and other people's time to create wealth for you. That's something you wouldn't have been able to do if you had to pay off all of the10 properties by yourself, using your own wages/income.

So, after all the mortgages have been paid off, you'd be getting your original $60,000 you invested back in rent *every six months*, and still have 10 properties!

Article
'Property Values'
by Graeme Fowler written in 2015

There are many different ways people use to determine what they think a property may be worth.

Here are some of them below:-

Purchase Price

RV, CV or GV (Rateable Value, Capital Value or Government Valuation)

E-Value (Desk-top Valuation)

Registered Valuation

Market Value

Looking at each of them, we can understand a little better what each is used for.

1. **Purchase Price** – this is the price you pay for a property when buying, and it may actually be worth more, or less, than what you are paying for it. Sometimes you may be in a multi-offer situation where you end up paying more than you originally intended to, or because you really like the property. Other times, it may be in need of work, or the owner wants to sell it quickly, so you may buy it for less than what it is really worth.
2. **Rateable Value, Capital Value or Government Value** – this is used for *rating* purposes and is a very rough guide to approximately what a property may be worth. In some locations, properties may *overall* sell on average for around the GV, and in other locations they may sell for approximately 20% or more above the GVs. In some instances, especially in Auckland recently, the CV can be at least $100,000 less than what a property will sell for. Also, you may buy a property that's run down and needs a lot of money spent on it, and then do a big renovation on it and it's now worth a lot more. The CV will still be exactly the same. The property is in most cases not viewed by the GV assessors, so is not something to be taken as a useful guide to establishing a property's true value.

3. **E-Value** – or desktop valuations are taken from an online system that calculates the values based on recent sales in the area. These can also be very inaccurate. It is generally used by banks as a guide for them to use, to determine approximately what a property is worth. These values can vary a lot depending on what the property last sold for, other recent sales nearby, and other data that is collected.

4. **Registered Valuation** – This is a valuation that you pay for, and is written up in a detailed report giving you comparable sales in the area. The banks will often use this to determine what amount of money they will lend you. Usually for rental properties it will be 80% of a registered valuation, and for a home you are buying to live in, they may lend you up to 90% of the registered valuation.
   Registered valuations can also vary depending on whether the valuation is for the vendor, or for the buyer. They can also vary a lot depending on the valuer. Some valuers will be conservative and use comparable sales to give you a *lower* figure as a valuation. And other valuers will be more generous, comparing the one being valued to *higher* sales in the area, resulting in a much higher valuation. I've seen valuations vary by 50% on the *same* property in the *same* week!

5. **Market Value** – This is the true value, or price that you would be able to sell the property on for again, if you had to sell it. This would be a willing buyer and willing seller in today's market. The market value changes over time, sometimes quickly, sometimes slowly. There is no *exact* market value for any property as it depends on how willing the buyer is and how keen the owner is to sell. It can also come down to who negotiates a better deal, also whether it is a private sale or sold through an agent. The salesperson's expertise in negotiating also comes into it, so there are several factors. However with a willing buyer, willing seller and each getting a fair deal, the market value would normally sit within a 3-5% range. For example, let's say a property is sold for $200,000 under normal circumstances – the true market value may be around $195,000 - $205,000.
   Generally, knowing the market value only comes from lots of experience, knowing the overall market very well, knowing other recent sales, and being totally immersed in what's going on in your area.

ARTICLE 'PROPERTY VALUES'

To give you an example of a couple of properties I purchased last year as buy and holds, here are the various values on each of them.

Property 1: -

a. Purchase price (including reno) $110,500
b. RV, GV, CV $122,000
c. E-Value $140,000
d. Registered Valuation $175,000
e. Market Value $150,000 - $155,000

Property 2:-

a. Purchase price $134,500
b. RV, GV, CV $114,000
c. E – Value $107,000
d. Registered Valuation $160,000
e. Market Value $145,000 - $150,000

The first property varies from a purchase price of $110,500 (including reno) up to a registered valuation of $175,000.

The second property varies from an E-Value of $107,000 up to a registered valuation of $160,000.

You can see by looking at all of these numbers above why a lot of people get so confused.

They all have a purpose. Whether the value is for the banks' use to determine how much they will lend to you; the local council's use for charging you rates on the property, or knowing for yourself what a property is really worth – by understanding and knowing *market* values very well.

ARTICLE

'The Best Question I Can Remember Being Asked by an Investor'

by Graeme Fowler written in Feb 2016

Question......

Because it seems like such a fine balancing act between expanding the portfolio versus paying down debt, I am keen to understand your view on the following: If you were to start all over again, would you allocate any extra funds left over at Year End (say, over five years) towards deposits for the next property purchases, or would you use it to pay down principal? And if used for paying down debt, would there be a certain LVR% that you might target before you start expanding again? I think your cash-flow strategy aligns closely with my values and goals, so I'm interested to see how quickly a sensible portfolio could grow.

....

Answer ......

Out of all the questions anyone has ever asked me in the last few years, I think that one has got to be the best one, so it deserves an equally good answer!

That level of thinking, your mindset and questioning will take you a long way, so good on you.

When starting out, you want to first of all *buy* well. Take the time to know the market really well before making any offers. Most people hope or *assume* that when they buy any property, the price will always go up. When I buy a property, I make the assumption that the market value will go *down*, so I want to make sure I buy really well. Then if the market values of the properties do drop, it doesn't matter too much to me.

So when starting out, if you can buy your first investment property at a good discount (not that easy to do in most locations right now, but definitely still possible), it will set you up well. If it was me, I would still finance it at 80% and work on ways to pay the debt down at no longer than on a 20 year P & I loan.

If the price goes up, do not borrow against any increase in value. That way of thinking and mindset will get you into trouble eventually. I only refinanced the 20 properties that I bought in 2014 as an experiment, and it was due to buying *well below* market value. I wasn't *hoping* for increases in market values later on. I also had a good solid foundation of around 40 properties before starting to do this.

So, with your first property, pay it down at a rate where you are not compromising what you would normally do with your fixed expenses, in other words, be sensible. With any extra money you receive, look at paying down the loan further.

Once you have paid the loan down to around 60 – 70% of the *price you paid* (not market value now) then you could look at borrowing again from that equity, but no more than say 75%.

So for example, let's say the property you purchased was $200,000 and your original loan was 80% of that ($160,000).

You could pay the loan down to say $130,000. Don't borrow any more than say an extra $20,000 now against that property (taking the loan now back up to $150,000 - which is 75% of original $200,000). That is, *unless* the market value has gone up greatly. Then you could borrow back up to the 80% again of the *original* purchase price. So that would be $30,000 you could then borrow, which you could use towards your next purchase.

N.B. The mistake most people make is by borrowing 80% on any increased value. So if it was now worth say $300,000 (up from the original $200,000 you paid), many investors would increase their borrowings up to $240,000 (80% of $300,000) and also have the next one leveraged at 80%, and continue on like that. So do not do that if you want to invest safely.

I would carry on like that, and always be slightly reducing your LVR each year.

But do this with the property values being the same as they were the *previous* year (12 months ago), not where they are now if they have gone up in value.

For example, let's say you have four properties with a value of $1 million and a debt of $700,000 (70% LVR).

In 12 months time, if the properties combined are now worth say $1.4 million and the debt is down to $650,000 you've been doing well to reduce the debt. Your actual LVR would now be around 46%.

However, if you borrow back up to 70% of the *new* value of $1.4 million, you would now have $980,000 borrowed. Then if the market prices dropped down to where they were in the *previous* year, you are now leveraged at an extremely high and very risky 98%!! ($980,000 debt with only $1 million of property).

So keep on paying down the debt as fast as you can, and make your position, or your foundation, stronger each year by reducing your LVR. Then when you do have occasional years that the market prices may go down, you aren't as exposed as many of the investors out there generally are.

Once you get more experienced, you may also want to do trades, renos etc for extra money.

N.B. When to trade/reno properties and when not to.

I've bought properties to trade in a rising market and then been stuck with them when the market has changed over a very short time-frame. Suddenly, there were hardly any buyers around and I couldn't sell the properties, so I ended up keeping them. Some were only recently changed into my original holding trust and the GST was paid back, this is now 10 years later. If the market is not declining like that (which can happen anytime without warning), it's better if you can buy properties that you can also rent at a reasonable yield, if the market does change. But it's a catch 22 situation as 'why would you not hold them to start with?' Sometimes you want the equity and sometimes you want to make some quick cash, and at times a property could be suitable for either a trade or a buy and hold. If you don't want to buy any more rentals at any point in time, then it's good to do trades for extra income, if you can.

But the other big thing is properties that don't fit within your investing rules for your buy and holds may be fine to trade or reno, and sell on again. These may be in worse locations than you would normally have your buy and holds in, or they could be more expensive properties that don't suit being rentals as the yields are too low, or some other factors they have that don't fit your rules and strategy for long term holds (for example, older character homes that may have too much maintenance to keep them as rentals). If you are doing trades or renos with these types of properties that don't fit into your buy and hold rules, then it's even more important to have other cash-flow available, if you do get stuck with them in a market that turns quickly. In that case it may be better to just sell at a lower price, and maybe even take a loss if you need to, in order to sell. Trades and renos can be very profitable as long as you know the market well, know your total costs, and know your end buyer requirements. Also making sure you don't go too much over your original budget, unless you are confident of getting that money back when you sell. After taxes (GST and income tax) are taken out, you lose about 40% of your profit, so it makes sense to focus more on your buy and holds when building your portfolio. But you may want to use trading/renovating properties and then selling them on, as an option to help create your new deposits for rentals, or in certain markets and certain situations.

This is what I did mostly in the early stages of building my property portfolio. The money generated from doing trades/renos was used for deposits to purchase more buy and hold properties. With all of those rentals that were purchased, I put in a 20% deposit. I didn't use any equity from any of the other properties that were being paid down, even though some of those original properties had doubled in value over two to three years.
The only time I ever did refinance a few properties was to borrow $200,000 to set up a business (franchise) back in 2002.

Hopefully by following all of this and with the mindset that you have, you will be very successful. Once you don't need any more wealth or you have all that you what you want in life, I think it's important to start giving back. If you've ever heard or read about Maslow's hierarchy of needs, you will know what I'm talking about here. If not, you can Google it and learn more. Basically once you have your basic needs and your psychological needs all met (food, water, warmth, shelter, safety, security, friends, intimate relationships, feeling of accomplishment etc), you may want to start giving back. This part is called self-actualisation. This is where your spiritual growth comes into it as well as giving back to humanity and to the world that helped support you up until this point. It's about *your* growth and *contribution*.

Hope that helps, thanks again for the excellent question.

Article
'Mindset'
by Graeme Fowler written in 2014

What do you think would be the biggest blocks to someone's success in real estate investing?

Some may say their lack of experience, or funding issues, possibly not having enough agents to find them good properties, and others may say it's the market itself – not doing what they want it to. All sorts of reasons as to what's stopping them from getting what they want.

These all sound like they could be valid reasons they believe are holding them back, but personally I think it all comes down to just one thing – their own *mindset*.

I believe someone's mindset and beliefs about certain things will either help them succeed, or prevent them from succeeding. When you have your mind set in a way that helps you rather than hinders you, everything seems to flow a lot more easily and effortlessly.

To give you an example of how this works, think of all the radio stations in your city that are now playing in the room, your car, work etc, wherever you may be right now. Even though you may not be able to hear *any* of them, it doesn't mean they are not playing – or transmitting. The reason why you can't hear them is because you aren't *tuned into* the frequency of any of those stations. If you were to *tune* into any of them, you could listen to whatever is being broadcast on each station, but only *one station* at a time. Now think of what *you know* to be true about *you* and the real estate market. This is your belief or set of beliefs, and the station *you* are tuned into.

Now to expand on it in more depth and the practicalities of it, think of it like this: - think of *yourself* as being the radio station being broadcast to the world. Realise now that only what matches *your* frequency that you are *emitting* – can be attracted to you. In other words, what you are putting out there can only attract what matches your transmission, your frequency, your output, your thoughts, your ideas, your behaviours and your beliefs.

For me, when I'm in a hurry to get somewhere, I usually get stuck behind some slow driver going 30 – 40km/h or get all red lights etc, and it ends up taking me longer than usual to get to where I'm going. That's because what I'm putting out there I'm bringing back or attracting to me. Similarly if I was in no rush to get where I was going, it would be a nice peaceful trip, most likely all green lights, people being courteous in traffic, all the things that I attract now because I'm in a peaceful and relaxed state of mind, and the time is not an issue.

A lot of people have beliefs about the food they eat, their own body, and their metabolism. How is it that two people can eat the exact same food, do the same exercises but get completely different results? What *creates* someone's metabolism rate, and what the body does with the food it receives? Let's say one person has the belief that they have created over time that food is their enemy and what they eat goes immediately on their hips, while the other has the belief that food is their friend and it's all good for them no matter what they eat. Do you think they will get different results over time?

You may have a belief that people are out to get you, take advantage of you, or you don't trust what others say to you, all sorts of beliefs about everything. And whatever they are – it must match what you believe, until the belief is changed.

For example, if you have the belief that it's hard to get finance to purchase more properties – only what matches that belief can be attracted to you. Or you may have the belief that – all the good properties always go to someone else before I get them. It must be true for you, or match your belief. It will stay like this until you can *change* that belief to a more empowering one.

A belief is a thought that you keep thinking over and over, and over, and over again until it becomes a belief and *your truth*. It's the same with any limiting belief, until you realise that the *belief* is what's holding you back, you will stay where you are. A new set of beliefs is what is needed to get you moving again, and on your way to where you want to go.

How do you change your beliefs? Some I've used in the past are affirmations or visualisations which can work well, but do take time. You also have to realise that *all* of your beliefs, whether it's about yourself, other people, work colleagues, your boss, salespeople, lawyers, accountants, religion, politics, relationships, health, money, losing weight, anything at all – it is only *your* point of view and not necessarily the truth. However because we've had these thoughts so often that end up *creating* our beliefs, we then attract everything that matches what we broadcast out there (our beliefs), and so we get more and more evidence to *prove to us* that our beliefs are really true!

There was a quote I wrote in my first book that went like this *"Many plane accidents occur because pilots' perceptions filter out and discard reality. An aircraft may be heading towards the ground, yet if the plane is level, he will ignore his instrumentation with a rationalisation that it is wrong. Similarly, juries are known to have made up their mind about a case usually by the end of the second day of a trial. What then happens is they filter out any new information that does not agree with their perceptions, and concentrate only on that which agrees with their biases. Individuals act as filters for all information they receive; each fact is measured against a set of personal, social, cultural or religious biases and then incorporated into an individual's consciousness. Everything we do is coloured by our perceptions and expectations. Information is always distorted, and if it doesn't fit our beliefs – it is discarded."*

Below I will use some statements (beliefs) about real estate investing and the emotions (frequency) that correspond to each belief. You could also use similar points of views/beliefs around money, health, relationships etc etc.

The top of the list goes from an equivalent emotion (frequency) of appreciation and empowerment, down to the bottom of the list to an emotion of despair, depression and fear etc.

1. Joy/Knowledge/Empowerment/Freedom/Love/Appreciation
   Money is abundant, I am appreciative that money always flows to me. Real estate is fun, easy, effortless and there are so many ways I can make money whenever I want to.
2. Passion
   I love doing what I'm doing, this is really what I want to be doing with my time.
3. Enthusiasm/Eagerness/Happiness
   I am enjoying the learning, learning is fun and I love doing this.
4. Positive Expectation/Belief
   I love doing what I'm doing, I am really expecting things to work out for me.
5. Optimism
   I am confident I'm moving in the right direction for me, things are going along well for me right now.

6. Hopefulness
   I am hopeful that what I am learning will give me all the information to succeed at this.
7. Contentment
   Right now, even though I would like more - if nothing changes for me, then I am happy exactly where I am.
8. Boredom
   I'm not getting much out of all this, in fact I find it a bit of a nuisance learning new things.
9. Pessimism
   It's alright for him, and for others, I don't have their confidence and I really don't think I could ever be like that, or do the things to be successful. It may work for others, but probably not me.
10. Frustration/Irritation/Impatience
    This is way too frustrating for me. I want things to happen now! Why can't I get the same sort of deals when I want them? It's really annoying to me.
11. Overwhelment
    This is all too much to take in, so many things I am supposed to learn. I don't think it's worth it.
12. Disappointment
    I missed out on several deals, the banks have said no to me. I feel stuck right now.
13. Doubt
    I'm doubting all of this now. It sounds good in theory, however I don't think it actually is true.
14. Worry
    Even if I do okay at this, I don't like debt and would be much too afraid of losing it all. There are so many things I keep worrying about, it is very stressful for me and not good for my health.
15. Blame
    My parents were poor and taught me having money was bad. They're the reason I am where I am today.
16. Discouragement
    Nothing I do seems to work out. I try really hard and never seem to get anywhere, what's the point of it all?

17. Anger
    I'm upset that some people have success and others don't, through no fault of their own. It angers me that some people have to work so hard and get very little for what they do.
18. Revenge
    I wish I was in government I would sort out those rich people and take all their money away, see how they like it. They should be taxed at a higher rate and give it to the less deserving like me. Why should they have it all and I always have nothing?
19. Hatred/Rage
    It really angers me this whole money concept, it's impossible to get ahead, the whole system is corrupt. The poor keep getting poorer while the rich get richer, it sucks big time.
20. Jealousy
    It's alright for him and all these others. I wish I had that too but know I never will, it's just not fair.
21. Insecurity/Guilt/Unworthiness
    My parents told me money is evil and they were right. I buy lotto tickets and hope one day I will win, and if I did I would give it all away to people who have nothing. Money only creates arguments. I would rather have nothing and be happy.
22. Fear/Grief/Depression/Despair/Powerlessness
    There is no point me doing anything, I feel powerless, resigned and tired. All I want to do is sleep all day and forget about the rest of the world. It's an evil world out there and I wish I could just go to sleep and never wake up.

So, whatever statement or statements are close to what your current beliefs are - *is where you are*. There's no right or wrong about it, it's just what is. What you want to ask yourself though is; this belief or reality I currently have – is it getting me to where I want to get, or is it limiting me in some way, or holding me stuck where I am?

Once you can identify that and be okay with it, accept it 100%, you can then start moving up the scale to where you would *like* to be.

As you get to each higher level, your *new belief patterns* will of course be *different*.

This in turn will attract to you whatever *matches* that new belief.

Ones mindset and what you 'give out is what you get back' is a huge subject and has taken me more than 10 years already to even begin to understand it. It all starts out with these two statements 'your power is in the now' and 'you create your own reality'. Even by beginning to know and understand this, your whole world can start to change for the better, and to what it is you really want, very quickly indeed.

Article

'Loan To Value Ratios' (LVR's)

by Graeme Fowler written in 2015

The LVR or loan to value ratio is a percentage that the banks use as one of the factors in determining whether they lend money to you, or not. They also take into consideration your personal income, rental income, other debts you may have, living costs and credit cards etc.

For the past few years, the LVR that most banks and lenders consider fairly standard is 80%. Recently this has been lowered to 70% for properties purchased in Auckland.

What this means is that if you're buying a property for say $500,000 and the bank's requirements is an LVR of 80%, then the bank will lend you 80% of the $500,000 which is $400,000. The other $100,000 will be in the form of savings or equity from your own home, or possibly other rental properties.

If buying the same property in Auckland with banks only willing to go to 70% LVR, they would lend you $350,000 and the other $150,000 would come from you.

Debt to Equity Ratio

This is often used by people thinking it means the same as LVR, but it is very different.

Debt to equity is a term more used in businesses to determine how much debt they have compared to equity in the business. To work out what the debt to equity ratio of a business is, you calculate total debt divided by total equity. So, if a company had $15 million in debt and total shareholder equity of $10 million, the debt to equity ratio would be 1.5 times or 1.5 to one (1.5:1)

Using it for property is not that common, although some commercial banks/ lenders may use it as a tool along with using the LVR.

What is a good LVR to have?

The banks are generally happy if your overall LVR is under 80% for residential property (70% in Auckland) until you get to a certain number of properties, or type of properties owned. The amount of properties can be different with each bank, and can also vary depending on the relationship you have with your bank, and sometimes if another bank wants your business.

Some banks will reduce your overall LVR down to 65% if you have say over five residential properties with them, others may have their limit at 10 properties and others may say it doesn't matter how many properties you have, as long as you have a good steady income from a job or a business.

Others may not be concerned about the number of properties you have, but the overall *debt* you have with them. Some will treat you as a commercial business (borrower) if you have over $1 million debt with them and some may say they will go up to $3 million of debt before you are treated as a commercial customer, and everything then goes to 65% LVR.

Often banks will be more cautious of investment properties you want to buy outside the area you live in. They may require a different LVR, or a registered valuation, and sometimes not lend to you at all. Also if the property you want to buy is under $100,000 some banks will be very wary of this and may limit you to a 60 – 65% LVR, or again not want to lend to you for this type of property.

Most banks will also treat a block of four or more flats as commercial, and therefore ask you to put in 35% as a deposit (65% LVR).

N.B. All commercial properties are generally treated as 60 – 70% LVR with the most common being 65%, so again a 35% deposit would be paid (or equity from elsewhere) to purchase any commercial properties.

Only a few years ago, banks were lending 90% and in some cases 95% on residential properties as well as rental properties, in other words a 90 - 95% LVR. The banks can change their rules at *any* time.

So, as you can see there are a huge amount of variables in all of this, and people will often think if their LVR is 80% or just under, they will always be safe. To me, that is not only wishful thinking, but also very risky.

My LVR is currently 57%, which means 43% of the properties I have are owned by me and 57% is still owed to the banks. The banks I deal with are very happy with this and say that the overall position and foundation of my whole property portfolio is now the strongest and most solid it has ever been. One said it was one of the most solid on their books throughout the whole of New Zealand! I was at first rather pleased with that, but then thought, really?

To me, there is still way more risk there than I am comfortable with and I want to get my LVR down below 50% as soon as possible. Ideally this will happen within the next two years by selling off a few properties (ones that were bought as trades several years ago) and paying down debt further. Eventually, the plan is to have my LVR at 0%, that is – no debt.

To me anything over 60% LVR if you have $5 million or more worth of properties has some risk. The higher your LVR is, obviously the higher the risk is.

This is what I would suggest as a guide for looking at your own LVR:-

Up to $1 million of property – 80% LVR

$1 million - $2 million – 70% LVR

$2 million - $5 million – 65% LVR

$5 million - $10 million – 60% LVR

$10 million - $15 million – 55% LVR

$15 million - $20 million – 50% LVR

Over $20 million – 40% or less LVR

What happens if the banks changes their rules?

This can happen at any time as we have already seen with Auckland properties now needing a 30% deposit as opposed to a 20% deposit for the rest of NZ. As mentioned there was a time not so long ago that banks were happy lending over 80% and in a lot of cases up to 95% on purchase price. Some 2nd tier lenders will still do this for those that want it or can meet their criteria. The interest rate is generally a few percent higher to cover their risk, and is not something I would recommend for any investors to use, unless the rules do change further and you can keep your LVR within the guidelines I suggested above.

If the banks changed their rules again to say for example, you now had to have 40% equity (a 60% LVR) across *your whole portfolio*, what would you do if you were now geared at 80%? You're only option would be to sell or come up with a large amount of cash from somewhere else. If a lot of people were in the same situation, property prices could fall drastically until people came into line with the new rule. Or if too many people were being forced to sell, the rules may eventually be eased once again.

To have a strategy of buying properties whenever prices go up, and always leveraging up to an 80% LVR, gets more and more dangerous the longer it continues.

Property is a long term investment, and not something you can get rich from over night. The higher your borrowings get up to, your LVR should keep coming *down* to safer levels as mentioned above.

Even though property is a long term investment, the rules and regulations can change very quickly. These can come from changes with the IRD rules, changes in government regulations for property, changes in bank requirements such as debt servicing, LVRs, or even higher interest rates being charged on investment properties.

What could happen to make the banks call in *your* loans?

I heard about an investor in NZ many years ago that had all 99 properties they owned with one lender, and that particular lender went into receivership. The properties were quite highly geared around 80% or so, and the investor couldn't refinance them in time with any of the other banks, and therefore all properties were sold at mortgagee auction, and he lost everything.

But could your bank call in all your loans? This is something that can happen to anyone at anytime. If you read the small print, a bank can ask for all their money back at any time.

It's unlikely that a bank would do this though without good reason. But there are many instances when they can ask you to reduce your *exposure* with them.

For example, they may think the properties you have mortgaged with them are now worth *less* than when they reviewed your portfolio the previous time.

This has happened many times to even very successful investors I know. All of a sudden the bank reviews your property portfolio and it shows up that a new E-Value for one of your properties is less than what is was the last time they did it.

They could ask you to get a new registered valuation, pay down some debt, or reduce the limit on any revolving credit accounts you have with them, just to bring it back into line with their rules. If you aren't able to do any of those things, they may ask you to sell your property or properties.

I've had times over the years when a bank has said to me that they were reducing the maximum limit on my revolving credit facility, because the values of some of the properties I had mortgaged with them, had dropped.

Even a small drop of 5 – 10% in value of your properties could have a significant effect on your overall position if you are too highly geared.

What can happen to change your LVR?

When I started investing over 25 years ago, I had saved $25,000 and the property I bought as a rental was purchased for $128,000. I also had to borrow another $10,000 to keep the bank happy, which was on interest only from a lawyer, just to make it work. In theory, my LVR was 80%.

The two loans totalled $103,000 ($93,000 bank plus $10,000 lawyer) and the $25,000 deposit was from my savings ($103,000/$128,000 ≈ 80%).

At the time I purchased this rental property, the bank had asked for a registered valuation. So I paid for a valuation and it came back and *said* the property was worth $128,000.

I say in theory, as I found out a little later on that the property was worth a lot less than the $128,000 I paid for it, more like $100,000. I eventually sold it for $98,000 several years later. This means if it was only really worth $100,000 at the time I bought it, my LVR was actually around 100%!

In this case, my LVR wasn't what I thought it was. If the bank had realised that as well, they could have asked for more money from me to bring my LVR back to a comfortable level, most likely they would have wanted around $20,000. At the time, it would have been impossible for me to do that as I was a mechanic on low wages and didn't have any spare money, let alone $20,000.

Apart from not knowing what your property is really worth if you had to sell it again (false valuations), there are a few other more obvious things that can change your LVR.

These will reduce your LVR:-

Paying down debt on your loans

Selling a property from your portfolio (unless there's more debt on it than you sell it for)

Values of your properties increasing

These will increase your LVR (and increase your risk):-

Borrowing money to buy more properties (80% +)

Borrowing money against property to live on, purchase vehicles, or buy other liabilities

Values of your properties decreasing

This may sound all rather scary to you, and potentially it can be very scary.

Or you might even think none of this will ever happen to you, and so you are in denial about the dangers of having high debts and a high LVR.

But hopefully you will realise that investing can be done with relatively low risk, by using a bit of common sense and also plan for what *could* happen. This could be from changes in rules or policies, property prices remaining static for long periods, or properties going down in value (which does happen at times).

Don't aim to get as close as you can to your banks' limits or rules. These can change at *any* time and by attempting to go to another bank - you might find their rules and regulations are even more strict.

Any small changes in the banks' policies, changes in law, your personal income, or any slight drops in property prices could affect you drastically. However it really doesn't need to affect you and shouldn't, providing you are sensible and have good money habits.

Safe investing.

N.B. Please read the 'Introduction' section at the front of this book if you haven't done so already. The part where I talk about the new LVR rules that have changed since this article was written.

Article

'What's The Real Estate Market Doing!!!!????'

by Graeme Fowler written in 2015

If you've ever played the board game Cashflow 101™ or Cashflow 202™, you will know that in order to win the game, the first thing you need to do is get out of the 'rat race'.

The 'rat race' in the game is a circle where you keep going around and around and around until you are able to get out onto the 'fast track'. This is where the game suddenly gets fast, exciting and a lot more money is made; but first you need to escape the 'rat race'.

How do you get out of the 'rat race'? You do so by getting to the point where your monthly cash-flow without your job (passive income) is greater than your monthly expenses. There are several ways inside the game to be able to do this; buying investment properties is one of them.

You will notice the game is called 'Cashflow 101', not 'Capital Gains 101'.

The 'capital gains' game is a game that most people who invest in property want to play. They think that prices will always go up and that it's a sure thing. Why shouldn't they?

Prices seem to increase about 10% on average every year and have done for the last 50 – 60 years, surely that's good enough for anyone? In theory yes, but it doesn't quite work that way.

Sometimes you will have years when the prices may increase 20% and other years it may be minus 10%. Market prices go up and market prices come down, just like the tide of the ocean comes in and then goes out. Warren Buffet has a saying that goes 'you can only see who's swimming naked – when the tide goes out'. How true is that?

Many investors have the idea or belief that some cities outperform others, when in reality any city with 100,000 population or more in NZ most often balances out over time in relation to all the other locations. If you look back to 50 or 60 years ago, the correlation between the 20 or so main cities in New Zealand back then is still very close to where it is now. It all balances out over time. As one area gets out of whack with the others, either with prices too high or too low, it doesn't take that long before it all balances out again. This is kind of what is happening in Auckland right now with demand being way higher than supply for the past several years. Now all the other main cities are experiencing huge growth while Auckland prices have been steadying. It's just what happens, and it will continue to do so as one area gets to be out of sync with other surrounding areas, as far as prices go.

The only difference has been that since the GFC in 2008, there haven't been enough new houses being built in Auckland, so prices have gone up more than they have done in the past. This may balance out again if there can be sufficient new houses being built, but it could take quite a few years still. It's supply and demand. If you have buyers competing for properties because there aren't enough houses for sale, it will push the prices up. When there are very few buyers around and lots of properties for sale, prices will usually come down as many vendors get more motivated to sell.

Another thing to consider about any future growth is that today, we are entering into something we haven't experienced for a very long time – low or possibly even zero inflation.

This could have significant effects on property prices – as in low to no growth for long periods of time. Especially if you compare things to how they've always been in the past.

With zero inflation, we may get many years of very little or even no price increase, nobody really knows for sure. Nor does anyone really know at any other time what the market will do from one year to the next, it's pure speculation and guesswork. Sometimes you will be right and think that you're a smart investor, and at other times you will be wrong and may even think you are stupid. Neither of these is necessarily true.

There are so many variables not only in our country, but things happening all around the world, that can affect us here in NZ.

Real estate investing is largely common sense and not something to think about as a short term get rich scheme. What the majority of people do when starting out is buy for the *hope* of higher prices in the future. This generally continues as they invest longer term, and so it becomes a habit. They are always trying to pick or guess what the market is going to do, and which locations around the country, or suburbs where they live, are going to go up in value more than others.

Then there are the short term thinkers, they get into property and hold for a short while. Prices may go up 10 – 20% and then they sell! What happens after that? Any profits they have made usually get spent on liabilities and consumables, not assets. Things such as vehicles, overseas holidays, or just general spending. Rather than selling their properties, if these people could think much longer term, they might wait until the tenants pay off their assets for them, and then have the cash-flow each and every week – plus still own the assets.

A good investor with low risk strategies and a good sound plan will not care too much about what happens in the future with property prices. Their focus will be more on buying well and buying properties that make sense – at the time they buy. It won't be dependent on their properties being worth more money in the future. Even if prices drop after they purchase them, it will not affect their investing significantly, and nor should it. If their strategy is sound, each and every property should stand on its own and take care of itself. That is, the rent should cover all outgoings on a P & I mortgage of no longer than 25 years, not an interest only loan. You may have to put in a 20% or more deposit to make this work for you, as far as cash-flow goes. It all depends on your yield. That is, the rent you receive annually, compared to the cost of the property you purchase.

There are three main ways to buy investment properties, and it all comes down to '*who* is paying for it', or the majority of it.

1. P & I loan (80 – 100% financed) – In this case the tenant is paying down the loan over time, not you. This is the ideal situation and when you do this, the price of the property going up or going down doesn't matter. You build equity each and every month by paying down the loan(s).
2. Interest only loan – Most of the time when people use I/O loans, they at least set it up so that the cash-flow will be break even for each property they buy. However the investor is reliant on the value going up on each property in order to build up any perceived equity. Nobody is paying the loan down; the tenant is merely paying interest on the investor's loan, or loans.
3. Negatively geared loan – Can be either a P & I or I/O loan. This is where the investor has a shortfall and needs to top up the mortgage every month. In other words, the tenant and the investor are both

paying the mortgage, or just the interest on the mortgage (I/O) and not paying off any of the debt. When interest rates go up, the situation gets even worse as the monthly mortgage payments will be higher on the loan, and now will have to be topped up even more.

The worst of all is a negatively geared loan on interest only.

The investor's only hope is that property prices go up more, rents increase, or interest rates drop further to help them. If any of these go the *other* way – that is market prices drop, rents drop (or there are unplanned vacancies/repairs and maintenance), or if interest rates go up, they could be in serious trouble.

What happens in a lot of cases is that things do work out in their favour for a while, it could even be 10 – 20 years that things all go well, and their *perceived* equity has grown exponentially. The problem however is that they keep borrowing up to a high debt level of say 80% or very close to it. And sometimes the valuations they get in order to borrow as much as they can are totally over the top. That is, they are often leveraged at higher than the 80% or so they *convince* themselves they are leveraged at. Sometimes they are 100%+ leveraged and don't even know it.

I think a lot of how this comes about is because people like to invest close to home, or at least in the same city where they live. This sounds reasonable and sensible, but it's only sensible if the properties they buy close to them are *suitable* as rentals. Also they should fit into the first example above of 'who is paying for it?'

Often the city where they live will not work well for investing. Yields are just too low. So they must choose a riskier strategy – because for them, investing close to where they live is of *higher importance* than having a good sound strategy that will work! They try to make it work, and it doesn't. Not immediately, but eventually it fails. That is, unless they are constantly reducing their LVR by paying down debt – and 95% who invest this way, do not.

Some investors in NZ are perfectly happy with a 4 – 5% yield and live in the hope of low interest rates forever, and ever increasing prices. In Australia, investors will happily accept 2 - 3% yields. These people will be in for a huge shock sooner or later. People have very short memories. Many people I know don't invest anymore because they got wiped out financially with only a small drop of 5 – 10% in market prices around 2007 – 2010. And that was when interest rates were going down!

For this typical type of investor, which is the majority of investors – their main focus, thoughts and attention is all about 'what's the market doing?'

They will say things such as 'this is a good capital gains area' or 'this is a potential good capital gains property' and talk as if it's an actual *real* thing!

If you read the property chat forums, or look at what the property coaches/ mentoring organisations are focusing on, or talk to real estate salespeople and read their news-letters and articles, read the news-papers, watch the News on TV, or even when you go out to socialise – people all want to talk about property prices! It's just so ridiculous, and it shouldn't matter at all.

I find a lot of the coaches and mentors are the worst culprits of all. Their whole livelihood depends on convincing their clients that they should 'buy as much property as they can, because property will only ever go up in value'. They are salespeople most of them, more than they are investors. Ask them where they make most of their money from – is it from investing themselves, or charging hundreds and hundreds of people $10,000 - $40,000 a year to mentor others? Many of them who coach or mentor others stopped investing a long time ago. Some of them have been lucky with market prices previously going in their favour, and so the newby, numpty type investors think they are smart and will therefore listen to them intently, and believe everything they are told.

So, going back to prices, if you're a private owner and simply wanting to sell your home and then buy another property, your property may have gone up in value, or not – just like all the other houses in your area would have done. There is no gain or loss either way.

Despite this, it remains the topic of conversation for so many people, even regular home owners. Even when I'm out walking each morning, I often hear people saying something like 'did you hear what so and so down the road from us sold their house for?!!'

And the investors who talk about it excessively continue do so, as their strategy for investing is so *risky* that everything they do with their investing is dependent on it. They often get very defensive if you tell them prices don't always go up, or say to them 'what happens if interest rates go up, or prices go *down*?' They can't hear it, or they block it out, thinking they don't have to worry about it, and it will never happen to them.

It would be like a game of rugby, or other such sport. Before the game, the build up wouldn't be all about talking of the actual game itself, but about the *weather* for the game! It would be endless and mindless chatter and commentaries about what the weather might be like for the rugby game. Will it be a nice day, will it be cloudy, will it be windy, will there be a chance of showers or rain, or possibly even snow? Nothing about the actual *game* itself.

That's how ridiculously stupid it is to talk about the prices of properties, and what people think might happen. It has nothing to do with the game itself, or investing. The market is just doing what it's doing and has always done, and there's nothing you or anyone else can do about it. There is no way you or anyone else knows from one year to the next what will happen, just like nobody knows what the *weather* will do from one week to the next. Sometimes it's fine, other times it rains, but it's *all* just weather! The same applies to property, sometimes it goes up in value, sometimes it changes only the smallest amount for many years and sometimes it goes down in value. It's just what happens, the way it is, and the way it always will be.

So knowing that, your role as an investor is to create a sound strategy that will work in *all* markets – not just some markets. Also a basic plan of how you are going to get there, and then look for the properties that will fit into those criteria.

As I mentioned, much of the time it may not be in the city where you live. It's usually outside the big main cities as the yields are often so low that it doesn't make sense to invest there. It only seems to makes sense if you're a speculative investor who likes to take big risks, and at the same time - think they are intelligent investors. In 95% of cases, they are not.

Do some people make it doing such risky things? Yes, but I've only ever met three or four people that have done so successfully over the long term. They are very smart people and keep their LVR low (60% or less), way less than the 80% that many investors do.

Before you even start to invest, ask yourself 'what do I want real estate to do for me?' Do I want just one or two properties that are eventually all paid off, and then live off the income from the rents? Is it to supplement my current income? Is it so I can eventually give up my day job? Or is real estate something I'm passionate about and want to make it something I do full-time and as soon as possible?

After you've done that, start to develop a low risk strategy to use in order to achieve what it is that you want. Not a strategy that relies on property prices going up in order for your plan to work. Having the belief that prices *always* go up and using that equity to keep on buying more, or selling half your property portfolio when it eventually doubles in value, or any other plan that involves prices continually going up - is *not* a strategy!!

When buying your very first rental, you want to buy well. Do your research and get to know market prices in the area very well - before you buy. Go out and look at 100 houses and find out what they sell for, and also recent previous sales that are similar to properties that you want to buy.

You only need one good deal to start. By buying well on your first property, it will set you up well for future purchases. If you don't buy well on your first one, it can cost you a lot of lost time (as well as money) like it did for me, seven years it was. So take your time to get to know the market well before you rush out and buy something.

In summary, stop talking about what you think may or may not happen with property prices, it's not what investing in property is all about. Focus on using strategies that work all the time, and in *all* markets.

Be an investor, not a speculator.

For me, if anyone asks the following questions – here are my answers:–

Do I know what prices will do from one year to the next? No

Do I care what prices will do from one year to the next? No

Does it matter to me what prices do from one year to the next, as far as investing goes? No

Do I care if prices in one location may go up more than another? No

Do I care what salespeople or news-papers or anyone says about the market, or what they think? No

Will the strategy I use work in all markets - up, down, or sideways for many years at a time? Yes

And that's all that really matters. ☺

PART 3.

20 Rentals in One Year

"When you are inspired by some great purpose, some extraordinary project, all your thoughts break their bonds: Your mind transcends limitations, your consciousness expands in every direction, and you find yourself in a new, great and wonderful world. Dormant forces, faculties and talents become alive, and you discover yourself to be a greater person by far than you ever dreamed yourself to be." Patañjali

THE IDEA: -

Talking to one of the agents I regularly use to buy and sell properties, something he said to me made me stop and think.

It was late 2013 and over the last six or so years, property prices in Hawkes Bay where I live, invest, and own most of my rentals had slowly drifted downwards about 20% in value. Some had dropped even more than that from the highs of 2006 – 2007, and only now in mid 2016 have prices come back up to where they were 10 years ago.

The salesperson mentioned to me that one of the younger investors in Hawkes Bay called Tom had a portfolio of nearly 30 properties, and he was only in his mid twenties. I thought 'how has someone so young bought so many properties already?' What he'd been doing was buying a few properties at mortgagee sale, others from highly motivated vendors, and also properties that needed work that he could fix up relatively cheaply.

I was told he was either a builder or had a builder friend that renovated these properties and then he'd revalue them and borrow against the increased equity. A few months later when I met him; it turned out he wasn't a builder, but had tradespeople do all the work. Tom has now become a good friend and we catch up regularly for coffees and chat about property.

So this thought of buying below value and refinancing, or buying, renovating and revaluing is one I had never done before, nor even considered. With all the properties I'd bought previously to hold as long term rentals, I would put in a 20% deposit and finance the other 80% over 20 years or so. Some of the earlier ones had been financed over 25 years, and depending on the interest rates and yields at the time, others were financed over 15 – 17 years. These deposits of 20% for each buy and hold rental were created mostly through trading properties. That is, buying low and selling at market price, or buying, renovating and selling. Tax has to be paid on all the profits on these trades so you actually end up keeping only around 60% of the total profit you made, after you've paid GST and income tax.

So this thought of refinancing went around in my head for at least a month or two, until sometime in December 2013 I had an idea. Starting in 2014, I would buy 10 properties over the next three years, beginning with one initial deposit of 20% which would come from equity in my *current* rentals. These properties would have to be bought well below market value, or significant value added through renovating. I would then get a registered valuation to show the bank what the new market value was, and then hopefully they would lend me 80% of that new *higher* value. Each property would then be refinanced giving me back my *initial* 20% deposit. The loan would be paid off on a principal and interest loan over 20 years. The rent would need to cover the rates, insurance, property management and of course the mortgage payments.

At the time, interest rates were around 5.75% - 6.00% p.a. fixed for 2 years, so I did my calculations on 6.5% p.a. In other words, the rent needed to cover all these expenses and allow for interest rates to increase up to 6.5% p.a. and still cover everything, or very close to it. I didn't allow for any vacancies or maintenance into these calculations, for a few reasons. They are a bit of an unknown and can vary from year to year, and I also wanted to keep things simple. I also had good cash-flow from my existing 40 rental properties that would cover any maintenance on these new properties being purchased, when needed.

By refinancing them like this, it would effectively mean that I would use no equity/cash after refinancing them if I could buy these 10 properties well enough. As an example of how I wanted it to work, a property that would now value to $150,000 – I would need to buy it for $120,000 (80% of $150,000) or less. The rent would have to cover the rates, insurance, property management and a mortgage of $120,000 on a 20 year P & I loan at 6.5% p.a. To get such a good deal was going to be very tough I thought. The yield I worked out at the time would have to be around 11% at least to make this work. All the other rentals I had ever bought had been around 8% – 10%p.a. yields. Usually the higher yielding properties of over 10%p.a. were in areas or streets that I would not want to own any rentals in, so it was going to be a real challenge.

To find *any* deals like this I thought was going to be extremely difficult, even with all my experience of buying more than 200 properties over the last 20 – 25 years.

Buying even one property like this I thought was going to be challenging enough, so I gave myself three years to buy the 10 properties. Each one would need to be bought around 80% of market value, and then refinanced in order to give back my 20% deposit. If this turned out to be successful, I would then have 10 properties all paying for themselves, and were 100% financed. In other words, no equity would be used from any of my other properties after all these properties were purchased and refinanced. They would be self-sustaining, apart from any maintenance and the occasional vacancy.

FINANCIAL INTELLIGENCE:-

You may have heard these sayings before "it takes money to make money", "you need money to make money" or "you need money first, in order to make money". While most people believe this, is it actually true? It is true for them as it is their belief. As mentioned in the introduction, a belief is something that you think over and over again, until it *becomes* a belief. Every bit of evidence you find from then on (unless your belief is changed) will always support this belief. In other words, you will never find evidence for something *outside* of what you believe to be possible. Your assumptions create the evidence for them. Evidence does not exist independent from your assumptions. *Evidence* does not lead to beliefs, *beliefs* lead to evidence.

Therefore if you really believe that you need money to make money, this has to be true for you.

Years ago I realised this wasn't true, you don't always need money to make money. It often takes just a bit of creativity and some sound financial intelligence. What I've found is that the lower your financial intelligence is, the *more money* it takes for you to make money. And in most cases even having a lot of money for someone with low financial intelligence, it is no guarantee for making any money.

That's why you will often hear about people winning a million dollars or more in lotto and then having nothing again, only a few years later. Apparently about 70% of the big lottery winners lose it all within five years of winning the money. Their mindset or financial intelligence does not change when they received the cash. And so it often doesn't take too long to be back at the point they were again financially, before winning the money.

In general terms, the lower someone's *financial* intelligence is; the harder it is for them to make money, even if they already have money. On the other hand, the higher someone's financial intelligence is, the less money they are likely to need, to make money.

Having studied finances, money, debt, compounding interest, leverage, and being able to use other people's money and time for many years now, I think I'm at a point now where my financial intelligence is reasonably high. It has taken the last 30 years of learning about money and finances and these types of subjects to get to this point. It's not something you generally just wake up one day with.

Having this now as my belief that 'you don't need money to make money', the idea of making money through property investing with effectively no money, it seemed like the perfect opportunity to put it to the test!

MY SON RYAN: -

Ryan was 9 years old at that time in 2013 when I had the idea. I was thinking if all this worked out how I planned it to, I could show my son Ryan how to do the same thing in another 10 years time when he was 19. That is of course, if he was interested. At that time he was way more interested in playing Minecraft on his iPad, playing soccer, and scootering. Now nearly three years later, nothing much has changed, nor much interest shown in property or finances. So I will wait and see what happens and leave it up to him as he gets older.

After 10 years if all this went according to my plan, I worked out there should be about $750,000 equity in the 10 properties if prices stayed the same. That is, if there was no capital gains over the next 10 years. However with a 3% increase in prices per year average, the equity would be now around $1 million. Also if prices dropped over the next 10 years, there would be less equity than $750,000 but equity would still be gained each month by using all P & I loans. I worked out that each month nearly $3,000 would be gained in equity over the 10 properties, or about $300 per property. This would increase very slightly each month over the term of the loans.

TALKING TO THE BANK MANAGER: -

The next step before I went any further was to talk to my bank manager and tell him what I proposed to do.

If you want to refinance any property that you buy, the bank will not normally let you do this for a minimum of six months after purchase, and some banks won't do this until 12 months after purchase. However if you've shown to have done considerable work to the property after taking possession, banks are usually willing to lend you 80% of a new valuation. Minor repairs and maintenance would not be included in this. It would consist of things like putting in a new kitchen or bathroom, new carpet and vinyl, painting the interior or exterior etc.

For me, I wanted to buy three or four rental properties each year for the next three years to give me my 10 rentals. This meant either renovating each property and adding value in order to refinance each property, or being able to refinance the properties quicker than the usual 6 – 12 months after purchase.

After talking to my bank manager and discussing what I wanted to do, he said they would allow me to refinance after only *three* months! It was really only because of a very long history with this bank and the fact that I had bought and sold many properties over the years. I had consistently proven to them that I was able to buy and sell properties on again, at a good profit.

The idea of using equity from existing properties in order to get the deposit for the first property was also talked about. What I wanted to do was use this deposit (20% of purchase price) to buy a property below market value, and then revalue it three months later, which would give me back this deposit. The same deposit would then be used for the next property purchased. This way I could buy up to four properties each year (one every three months), and maybe even more if major renovation work was done.

This was great I was thinking. It all seemed like it could actually work!

Then my bank manager Mark said to me "to make it even easier, we could finance these properties at 100% of purchase price for you, and then release the equity that was used three months later. That is, once they've had registered valuations on them".

This was a bit of a bonus and meant that rather than using the one deposit and recycling it every three months, I could buy other properties if they became available within that three month time frame. This made good sense to me as it would mean that if I was able to find two properties or more that fitted my criteria before the three months was up, I could buy both of them, rather than buying only one.

At the time I was thinking it's going to be difficult enough just to buy one property at such a big discount every three months, let alone two or more. But it was a bonus having that available if required at any stage over the next three years.

NEW TRUST:-

Rather than putting these new properties into my existing trust with around 30 rentals in it already, I thought it would be a lot simpler and easier to track them if I set up a new trust for these 10 properties. That way, I could easily see what was happening on a daily basis with my property spreadsheet that I've used for many years. Having a separate entity, it would make it easy to see the total loans and values of these properties, the total equity, the total rents, the total mortgage payments, rents after expenses (rates, insurance and property management), and the equity gained each month by paying off principal.

Even though there was the extra expense of setting up a new trust, it made sense to do so, so I asked my lawyer Chris in Wellington to set it up for me. The new trust was to be called 'Andorra Holdings Trust'.

ORIGINAL STRATEGY:-

My strategy for all the previous rental properties I had bought was to always start by purchasing them well. This would typically be around 5 – 10% below market value. In other words, buying them at a price I was confident of selling them for more, if I needed to. I would always put a 20% deposit into each new rental property. This was made from either trading, or buying, renovating and selling properties – in my trading company. The loan would be then paid off over somewhere between 15 years and 25 years, but never any longer. The term of the loan depended on the yield, the interest rate at the time, and how my overall cash-flow was looking. If I didn't have a lot of cash-flow I would make the term longer, if there was good cash-flow then the loan term would be shorter. The majority of the loans on my buy and holds were taken out over 20 or 25 years, and only five or six loans were for less than 20 years. After financing each property, no matter what happened to property prices after that – whether they went up or down significantly in value over time, the plan was to never refinance them.

The only time in all my years of investing that I ever did refinance a few properties was when I needed $200,000 at fairly short notice in mid 2002, when I decided to buy the Mr Rental Franchise for Hawkes Bay. I refinanced four or five loans in order to do this, but kept them on the *same loan term* which of course made the loan repayments higher. Often people will refinance their properties and also extend out the term of the loans, meaning they will pay a lot more in interest than they originally planned for.

N.B. This is very common when people buy their first home to live in and let's say take out a 25 year mortgage. Several years later they may have a family or want something with more space, so they decide to sell their first home and buy a new one. What happens when they come to buy the new home and take out a loan to purchase it? In almost all cases they pay the original loan back and take out a new loan, again for 25 years (or the same term as their original loan). If they've been paying the original loan for five to seven years, most of their payments have been going to pay the interest on the loan, and not a lot of principal has been paid. So when they pay back the original loan, the original balance usually hasn't reduced by that much.

The value of their home may have gone up significantly over the time they've been living there, so they may feel like they've made up for it in that way, and it doesn't matter so much. They may be thinking 'we've made $50,000 or more just by living here over the last five years, and that makes up for all the interest we've paid'. And so they feel like they are smart with their money and make good financial choices.

The problem with that is all the other houses around them have also gone up in value. So they take out a 25 year loan for their new home and start paying the mortgage on this one. Their original plan may have been to have no debt on their own home by the time they are age 50. This has now been extended five to seven years by taking out this new loan. Now they hope to be debt free by age 55 – 57.

Another seven years or so goes by and they decide to sell again and buy something else. This time it's a nicer home, a better part of the city, and better zoning for their kids' school. Again not much principal has been paid off the loan, but it doesn't matter they think, as again the value has gone up over the time they've lived there. They go out and buy the new home by paying back the loan on their last house, and now take out a new 25 year loan for this one. This can go on several times over people's lifetime and each time the original date they planned on being debt free on their home, gets extended out several more years. This is one of the biggest reasons why people still have a mortgage on their own home when they want to retire.

What could they have done instead? Rather than taking out a new loan each time they bought a new home, look instead at the original end date on the loan of the first property. Let's say when they bought their first home they took out a 30 year mortgage. In seven years time they want to buy something bigger, so decide to sell up and move house. The original loan would still have had 23 years remaining on it before it would have been paid back in full. With the loan on the new property, rather than taking out a new 30 year loan and paying mostly interest again, make this one for a maximum of 23 years. If they cannot afford the payments on a 23 year loan, then don't buy it! By doing this they will save thousands and most likely hundreds of thousands of dollars in interest over their lifetime. Each time they want to buy a new home, keep the original term or end date of the original loan the same. In other words, if they want to sell in another five years after buying this second home, the original loan term would now be down to 18 years remaining. Make the new loan term on their third home for 18 years. Keep doing this each time they move, and then 30 years after taking out their original loan, they will have no mortgage on their own home.

This is really important to understand; and also to understand how mortgages work and the amount of interest you pay – especially in the first few years of a long term loan.

NEW STRATEGY:-

Buying these 10 properties the way I planned on doing would require a slightly new strategy to how I had done things in the past. Some parts of the original strategy would remain the same or similar, firstly to buy these properties below market value (although now it needed to be around 20% below rather than 5 – 10%). The loan terms on the properties were now all to be 20 years, and as usual, never refinance again after each loan was in place.

The differences with this new strategy were; first of all I didn't need a deposit as I was initially obtaining this from existing equity in other properties, and secondly I would need to get a registered valuation three months after purchase, in order to release back the equity to my existing properties that I used as security.

Again, to make the valuation part of this even easier I had another idea. Rather than disturbing the tenants to have a valuer go through each property three months after buying each one, I would get them valued at the time of *purchasing* them. If you have a real estate salesperson or a valuer organised to go through one of your rental properties, the tenants will often get very suspicious and may think the landlord now wants to sell, and so it can make them rather uneasy about this.

So, the bank was happy for me to have a valuer go through the property when I purchased them, do a valuation, and then three months later do a roadside inspection of the property and take a new photo. This had the added bonus of the valuer not knowing what I had paid for each property.

What often happens is that you may want to get a valuation done on a property say 6 – 12 months after you've purchased it. The valuer will be able to look up the stats and see how much you paid for it back then. And so, if you had bought really well six months earlier and the overall market prices were still much the same as they are now, this can influence them to a certain degree with their thoughts on what value they will put on it.

For example, you may buy a rental property for $300,000 that has a market value of $375,000 (20% below market). The bank would most likely have lent you 80% (or 70% in Auckland) of the purchase price of $300,000 at the time which is $240,000 ($210,000 Auckland).

You now decide because you bought it so well that you want to reuse that equity if you can, and so ask a valuer to do a valuation on the property. Seeing that you only paid $300,000 six months earlier could easily influence their thoughts on price, even if in their own mind the property is most likely worth $375,000.

This meant for me, that being able to get the valuation done at the time of each purchase when the valuer *didn't know* what I was paying for it, was very beneficial.

This was assuming that I would be able to buy something at 20% below market value, *and* there was not any renovation work needed to be done to the property. If any renovation work was needed to be done after purchasing a property; this would all be completed first, and then get a registered valuation. All of this would still happen before a tenant moved into the property and rent it.

A REALISATION: -

It must have been a few days after I met with my bank manager Mark and talking to him about my new plan and strategy that I had an interesting realisation. Only a month prior to all this which was in December 2013, I had bought a property through one of the real estate companies in Napier. The property was a 3brm home with a large garage on a 620m2 section in Onekawa, Napier. I purchased it in my trading company and it was the eighth or ninth property I had bought in 2013 to buy and sell on again. Some of the properties I had bought in 2013 were sold on to other investors that I know, and three of them were renovated and sold on through the local real estate agents I deal with in Hawkes Bay.

The Onekawa one I had settled on in December could have either been a buy and hold, or a trade. Many times when buying properties over the last 18 years or so, a property that was being purchased could have suited being a good trade; and equally as good, a buy and hold. It usually depended on if I wanted a rental property more at the time – and also have the equity available to do this; or more wanting the *cash or equity* at the time, and hence a quick profit. Buying all the long term rentals in the past had required a 20% deposit which was created mostly from trades and renos.

At this time in 2013 and over the previous eight years, I had only purchased six buy and holds. Three of these were in one purchase in 2007, they were 3 x 2 brm flats in Hastings that I bought at auction.

Much of the time from 2006 – 2012 was a consolidation period for me and so not very much activity at all in the property market. It was also not a great time to be trading properties; nor was it a good time to be renovating and selling them as there were very few buyers around at that time to sell them to, in a declining property market.

By the time 2013 came around, things had pretty well stabilised in the property market in Hawkes Bay, so a fairly even amount of willing buyers and willing sellers for the first time since 2006 – 2007.

The Onekawa property was just another quick trade to be completed, just like the previous ones I'd started to do again that year. I would make some money on it and that would just help reduce a bit more debt.

At that time my LVR (loan to value ratio) was almost exactly 50%. I had been working on reducing this as best I could, and was now very comfortable with that level. It's not that easy to reduce your LVR in a *declining* property market. As property prices are slowly dropping like they did, the debt you owe on them doesn't reduce unless you are paying it down, and so your LVR is actually increasing.

So, what was the realisation with the Napier property I'd recently traded, only a few weeks earlier than wanting to start this new idea and plan? It was that this property I'd just sold would have been a perfect one that fitted everything that I was looking for! The purchase price had been $141,000 through an agent in Napier, and I sold it privately a couple of weeks later for $170,000 to another investor. It would have rented for $310 a week giving me a yield of 11.4% p.a. Borrowing the whole $141,000 purchase price and paying the mortgage over 20 years at an interest rate of 6.5%p.a, I worked out that it would have been still about $1.00 a week positive cash-flow. This was after paying the mortgage, the rates, insurance and property management. Interest rates in early 2014 were around 5.75% p.a. fixed for 2 years, so it would have actually been about $15 a week cash-flow positive after all these expenses.

It was also purchased for around 20% below market value. It would have only needed to value to about $175,000 which would have meant I could have borrowed the full amount of $141,000 and still be seen by the bank to be borrowing 80% of market value. It would have been a perfect property to start with, and was in a great location.

Even though this property was an exceptional and unusual buy, I thought it may well be possible to find 10 deals like this over the next three years.

Every property purchase is different and people sell their properties for such a wide range of reasons, some being more motivated than others. This purchase was very unusual, as it's not that often that you can buy a property through an agent and then sell it privately for more money only a couple of weeks later. Occasionally agents will get their pricing slightly wrong, or vendors will list their property at a lower price to get a quick sale.

This one was listed for $159,000 which was already below what I knew it was worth. But if I had paid that much for the property, it wouldn't have been a good trade. For it to be a good buy for me, I knew I would have to pay no more than $145,000. That way, if I'd sold it through a different agent for say $170,000 and paid their commission for selling it, also the holding costs for a couple of months and legal costs for both buying and selling, I knew there would still be a profit of at least $10,000 minus tax.

Knowing that $145,000 was the most I would pay, my initial offer was $137,000 subject to my usual three days finance clause.

The property was new to the market and so my offer was the first one submitted. Because the family wanted to move away from Hawkes Bay, they were quite keen to sell and move fairly soon.

The salesperson called me back the next day and said the vendors haven't countersigned my offer as now there was another offer coming in on the property. Often when this happens, I withdraw my offer as I don't like to be in competition with other buyers (unless it's at an auction where it's unavoidable), and I also know that the other offer is likely to be higher than mine. On this occasion rather than pull my contract out, I decided to just go a little bit higher than my first offer, and make it cash. So I increased the offer to $141,000 and signed a multi-offer form to say I knew I was competing against another buyer.

The salesperson called me a day or so later and said they had accepted my offer. I was quite astounded and asked what happened. Apparently the other purchaser had decided not to make an offer after all.

Interestingly enough, I found out a few months later from another salesperson at the same company why they hadn't submitted an offer. This salesperson had them as his buyer, and the reason why they didn't offer on the property was because they thought their offer would be too low, and so they would miss out. They thought they would be wasting their time and also the salesperson's time. Then he told me that their offer was going to be $155,000!

I don't know if he ever told his buyer that the property had sold for $141,000 but I can imagine they would have been rather annoyed at themselves for not offering on it, had they known.

So remembering about this property, it showed me that it may well be possible to find 10 similar deals to this one over the next three years. Properties I could buy at 80% of what I knew they would value to, and the rent would cover the mortgage, rates, insurance and property management.

PROPERTY NUMBER 1
BIRKENHEAD CRES, FLAXMERE

After having the realisation that the property I had bought and sold only a month earlier from starting on this new plan and strategy, I had another realisation!

I had settled on another property in late 2013 which was bought at mortgagee sale. The plan was to have it renovated and then sold on again, just like the others I had already done in 2013. This one was a 4brm home in Flaxmere, Hawkes Bay with double garage on a 767 sqm section, and was bought for $127,500. The mortgagee auction was actually in November 2013 and had the settlement several weeks later.

By the time I had the idea of buying 10 properties and recycling the deposits, renovations had already been started on this property. Not a lot had been done in the way of renovations though by early January 2014, as it had settled fairly close to Christmas when it's often not that easy to get a lot of work done.

The second light bulb moment or realisation I had was that this property I was having renovated might also have made a good first property for the new trust. It had never occurred to me before this as I had settled it in my trading company and was focused on having it renovated and then sold on again.

My thoughts were that I would spend about $15,000 on renovations and then sell it on again at a profit. Including renovations, holding costs, legal fees etc I estimated the property would owe me about $145,000 and should be worth about $180,000. If I sold it through an agent I would end up with just over $170,000 and a profit of approximately $25,000. By the time you take GST and tax out of that, I would have been left with around $15,000.

After having the thought that this may work as my first property for the new trust, I worked out some numbers and also called my accountant Tony in Wellington. After working out how much rent I would get, compared to the expenses of a mortgage on a 20 year loan, rates, insurance and property management, it looked like it could work okay. Tony said I could sell it from my trading company to the new trust if I wanted to, and the purchase price would be the after renovated cost. The only downside was that when I did eventually sell the property even if it was 30 years later, I would still have to pay tax on any profit. To me, that wasn't really a big issue.

So overall I thought this sounded great and decided that's what I would do. It also had the bonus of keeping the property and having tenants eventually pay off the mortgage for me, as opposed to ending up with only around $15,000 after tax as a trade.

Another few weeks later near the end of January 2014, renovations were all complete and I had spent a total of $15,300. This included putting in a good 2nd hand kitchen, painting the interior and some of the exterior including the garage, new carpets, new vinyl, and some other minor repairs and maintenance around the home including some gardening work.

All up including renovations the property owed me $142,800 (I didn't include holding costs or legal fees) and so that is what the new trust purchased it for. A tenant was found fairly quickly by my property manager and was rented for $320p.w.

I worked out on my property purchase calculator that even at an interest rate of 6.5% p.a. it was still $3.00 a week positive cash-flow, after expenses. With the interest rates being around 5.99% p.a. at that time, it worked out to be $13 per week positive cash-flow.

The next step was to get a registered valuation on the newly renovated property. I really needed it to value to at least $178,500. This was in order for me to borrow 80% of that valuation which would then give me the $142,800 I wanted. I could then recycle my initial deposit and renovation costs, and effectively make this property my first "no money down deal" in the new trust.

In other words if the property valued up to where I thought it would, the bank would be happy to lend me 80% of the valuation, meaning I would have used no equity to buy it (after the refinance), and the rent would still cover all the expenses on a 100% bank loan over 20 years.

The valuation ended up coming back at $190,000 which was even better than I was hoping for. The bank was happy to lend 80% of this valuation which worked out to be $152,000, or just over $9,000 more than what the trust paid for the property. I didn't need to borrow any more than the $142,800 that was required, so all it did was create an extra $9,200 of equity available in the eyes of the bank to use for my other properties if ever needed.

I was now on my way to my goal of buying 10 properties this way, with no equity being used after the refinance.

PROPERTY NUMBER 1

This first property turned out even better than that, as it had strengthened my overall property portfolio position by giving me back $9,200 of equity after the refinance. Or, if another property was purchased in the new trust where the valuation didn't quite come up to where I hoped it would, there would be $9,200 available in equity to make up for that shortfall.

PROPERTY SUMMARY: -

4brm home, garage

Purchase price: $142,800

Rent: $320p.w.

Yield: 11.65% p.a.

Interest rate: 5.99% p.a. fixed for 18 months

Loan term: 20 years

Loan Type: P & I

Cash-flow positive/negative: $13p.w. positive *(after the mortgage payment, the rates, insurance and property management)*

PROPERTY NUMBER 2
KINGSLEY DRIVE, FLAXMERE

It didn't take that long to find my next property. It was around the same time that the first property was being finished that one of the salespeople I deal with in Hastings called me. It was another property in Flaxmere, a bit further down into the suburb, but still in a location that was suitable for buying good rental properties in.

There are 10 – 12 streets in Flaxmere that I avoid for long term buy and holds, but they can be suitable for a trade if bought well, or a renovation and sell on again. Many investors do buy in these streets that I won't buy in as a long term hold, and some still do well with them if they have good property management in place. But overall the streets to me are more risky long term, so I avoid buying in them for my long term property holds.

This property was on the market for $159,000. It was a 3brm home, fairly tidy condition, a garage and good sized section. I estimated it needed maybe $1,000 - $1,500 spent on it to bring it up to a good standard to rent out the property. It was an owner occupied home and had been on the market for a while and had not sold. I thought it should value to about $155,000 or maybe just over with a registered valuation, and its market price would be around the $150,000 mark. For it to work for me, I would need to buy it in the high $120,000's which seemed to me at the time very unlikely. However the salesperson let me know that if it didn't sell soon it would possibly be going to a mortgagee sale, and as it turned out there was another real estate "for sale" sign put up at the property only a couple of days later. The other company had been instructed by the bank to sell the property as a "mortgagee", whereas the *vendor* had instructed the agent I was dealing with, to sell it.

This can happen at times in similar situations. The vendor wants to keep a good credit rating and not be forced to sell by their bank at a mortgagee sale, so they list their home with a real estate agent. Often what happens though is because they owe more money on the mortgage than what the property will sell for; they list the property for sale at a price which most buyers are not prepared to pay for it. And if buyers do make a lower offer, the vendor isn't able to sell the property because the amount of money owing on the mortgage, is higher than the offer. Plus they still have real estate agent's fees and legal fees to pay.

I ended up putting in an offer for $127,000 and made it a cash offer. Normally I will put in a three day finance clause in my offers to start with, but because of the situation with the other real estate company and the bank now being involved, it was best for me to go cash. The offer was presented to the vendor; however she wasn't able to accept it or sign it even if she wanted to, as there was more money owing on the mortgage, than my offer. The offer therefore had to also be presented to her bank. The bank would need to decide if they were likely to get a better sale price through the other real estate agent that they had instructed to sell the property at mortgagee sale, or my offer. As it turned out, two days later the salesperson called me and said the bank had accepted my offer. They had decided to accept it and not risk the property selling for a lower price at mortgagee sale.

The property ended up renting for $280p.w. and the valuation came out at $165,000 which again was more than I was thinking it would. If you take 80% of the registered valuation figure of $165,000 you get $132,000. The bank therefore would have been prepared to lend me $132,000 to buy the property. The purchase price was $127,000 so it created another $5,000 of *available equity* to borrow if I needed it for future purchases. I could have borrowed a little bit extra to do the repairs and maintenance that cost $1,500 before the tenant moved in, but chose not to. The bank was also giving me $1,000 and sometimes $1,500 upon settlement for taking out each loan with them.

Property number 2 was now underway and it was only early February!

PROPERTY SUMMARY: -

3brm home, garage

Purchase price: $127,000

Rent: $280p.w.

Yield: 11.45% p.a.

Interest rate: 5.99% p.a. fixed for 18 months

Loan term: 20 years

Loan Type: P & I

Cash-flow positive/negative: $2.50p.w. positive

PROPERTY NUMBER 3

TENBY TCE, FLAXMERE

It was only a week or two later that Jason and David who had just sold me Property Number 2, called me about another property in Flaxmere that had only just been listed. They now knew what I was looking for and thought it may be suitable for what I wanted. The property was very clean and tidy, and nothing needed to be done in order for it to be rented. It had been a 2brm property with a garage, but the garage had been converted into a third bedroom at some stage. Being on a corner section, it had two driveway entrances. The driveway around the corner led to a carport, so the lack of a garage which had been made into a bedroom wasn't such an issue. The vendor for this property had been selling a few of his other properties and was keen on a getting a clean, quick sale. It all happened very quickly and easily and we agreed on a price of $110,000.

My property manager found a tenant that was happy to pay $270p.w. which made the yield an extremely good one at 12.76% p.a. The other two properties I had recently purchased had yields of over 11% p.a. which was still excellent, and higher than any other properties I'd ever bought to hold as long term rentals. The registered valuation came in at $135,000 which was about where I was expecting it to, 80% of that being $108,000. With the purchase price being $110,000 it simply meant that $2,000 of the extra $14,200 that had been created in the previous two properties ($9,200 and $5,000) was now in credit by just over $12,000.

By this time it was still only mid February and already I had found three properties that fitted exactly what I was looking for. My original plan had been to buy 10 properties over three years like this, as I really thought it may take that long to find such deals. Now it looked like I may be able to find 10 properties in less than one year!

PROPERTY NUMBER 3

PROPERTY SUMMARY: -

3brm town-house, carport

Purchase price: $110,000

Rent: $270p.w.

Yield: 12.76% p.a.

Interest rate: 5.99% p.a. fixed for 18 months

Loan term: 20 years

Loan Type: P & I

Cash-flow positive/negative: $21p.w. positive

PROPERTY NUMBER 4

BESTALL ST, NAPIER.

Up until this point, the three properties I had purchased in the new trust had all been in Flaxmere, Hastings. Also most of my other rental properties were either in Hastings or Flaxmere, with only three out of the 40 or so properties I owned being in Napier. It was an area I knew okay but not that well, and I didn't know market prices quite as well as I did in Hastings or Flaxmere.

A friend of mine had mentioned this one to me and so I called a couple of salespeople in Napier that I had bought properties through previously, and asked their thoughts about the location and price. The vendor wanted $115,000 which sounded very reasonable to me and the salespeople also said if the property was okay inside then that would be a great price.

I went over the next day and had a look. It was a solid and fairly tidy 1960's 3brm home with a garage, and situated on a 650sqm section. There was already a tenant paying $260p.w. that had been there quite some time and wanted to stay on if the property was sold. The property needed a few minor things to tidy it up so I allowed $2,000 to get the work done. The street had also improved in appeal fairly recently and it had really helped the area. Very close to this home there used to be a block of four very run down two-storey state-houses, and they had been pulled down about five years earlier. It was now a nice park and it had really helped make the whole area more appealing, and a lot easier to attract good tenants. At $260p.w. rent, the yield was just over 11.5% p.a. taking into account the additional maintenance and repairs. Because it was such a good price, I agreed to it and didn't negotiate on it at all.

N.B. I remember an incident quite a few years back when buying a property privately, something I will never forget. It was an out of town vendor who had contacted me and was in Hawkes Bay doing some work on his property, renovating it one weekend with his family. It was in a great street in Hastings and they were most of the way through renovations on it. Then when it was finished they were going to sell it. He wanted $135,000 once the property was complete, which sounded about right to me at the time. I went over to see the house, and then chatted to the owner after having looked *through the property. We chatted briefly about the price and the settlement time-frame that he would like if I bought it. I asked him how much he would take for it 'as is' and I would get the tradespeople I use to finish it all off. That way they could finish up now and not have to complete the painting and other minor work they were doing. He seemed very keen on that idea, but wanted to think about it and talk it over with his wife for a couple of hours first.*

So I left and then called a salesperson I knew well and asked him about the property. He said "if you can get it for $135,000 even as it is now, it would be a great deal, just buy it Graeme". It all sounded good to me, so after a couple of hours I phoned back and his wife answered the phone. She said her husband was busy painting so I could talk to her about the price. I asked what price they had come up with after chatting about it. She said they would take $127,000 for it 'as is' and I could come around now with a sales and purchase agreement and they would sign it. I thought, wow that is a great deal! But rather than agreeing to the first offer which is something I don't often like to do, I said "how about $126,000, would you accept that?" She asked her husband and he said "no, and now the price is $135,000 if he wants it!!" I said "okay, look I will pay the $127,000 – I'm happy with that." Her husband then got very angry and again said "no, the price is #$@&%! $135,000 and I could take it or leave it". I was quite stunned by this and also very disappointed about missing out on such a good deal for the sake of only $1,000. It was a good lesson for me though about not trying to push for every last dollar in negotiations. This deal had cost me a lot of money by missing out on it, only because I was trying to push for another, what would have been insignificant amount of $1,000.*

I told a friend of mine who was also an investor about what had happened a few weeks later, and he asked if he could call the owner to have a look at the property. I said yes that was fine, but please don't mention that you know me! He ended up buying the property for even more money, paying $150,000 for it which I thought was quite a high price to pay. I was proved wrong though as he sold it six months later for over $200,000!

This experience taught me well about listening more, not going for every last dollar, and to be better at reading situations.

With the Napier property, I therefore decided to pay the asking price of $115,000 as it was already a good deal. After getting the few repairs and maintenance done it would cost me approximately $117,000 in total, which I was very happy with. The deal was signed up and I organised a mortgage on the property with my bank for $117,000.

The property valued to $150,000 with the registered valuation, meaning the bank could have lent me up to 80% of this amount, or $120,000. Again, the extra $3,000 that could have been available if I had paid $120,000 for the property was stored as an *equity credit* to add to the previous $12,000, making it now $15,000. All this really meant was that if I bought a property that didn't value to what I hoped it would, there was some extra equity available there now. In other words, there was now $15,000 extra equity in the eyes of the bank if I needed it. Remember my original plan was to use 'no equity' to purchase these 10 properties, and so far I was $15,000 in credit, or ahead of that target.

PROPERTY SUMMARY: -

3brm home, garage

Purchase price: $115,000

Maintenance/repairs: $2,000

Total cost: $117,000

Rent: $260p.w.

Yield: 11.56% p.a.

Interest rate: 5.75% p.a. fixed for 18 months

Loan term: 20 years

Loan Type: P & I

Cash-flow positive/negative: $3p.w. positive

PROPERTY NUMBER 5

FLEMING CRES, NAPIER

This one was more of an unusual purchase. It was originally a 3brm home with garage and a sleep-out, and had been converted by the current owners into a 2brm home with an extra large lounge. Because it also had a sleep-out off the garage, it still had three bedrooms available to use if people wanted.

It was next door to a property I had already owned for more than 10 years, and it was a mortgagee sale. The owner also wasn't letting anyone through the property to view it, including all the agents. Even the listing agent hadn't been able to get through inside to view it.

The tenants in my property next door had been there for all the 10 years that I had owned it, and had been there for at least a couple of years before I purchased it. I knew them quite well as I'd managed the property for a while before getting property managers to manage all my properties in 2004. So I called them and asked if they knew the owners next door, and also asked to check if it would be okay for me to have a look through the property. I said I may be able to keep them on as tenants if I bought the property, or if they didn't want to stay on, I could offer them some money towards moving costs.

It turned out they did know the owner reasonably well, and so arranged for me to look through the property a few days later. It was all very tidy, well looked after and a lovely home. The owner did want to stay on if the property was sold, and so I said I would keep him on as a tenant if I bought the property at the mortgagee sale.

The current owner had bought the property almost 10 years before this for $165,000 and I knew if I could buy it for anything less than $125,000, I would be doing very well. My estimation of the market price was around $150,000 and it should value to that much comfortably I thought, maybe even a little more.

A few weeks later the auction came around, and as far as I know, no other buyers had been able to go through. I'm not sure if even the salespeople had ever got through to view the property either.

Being a mortgagee sale, it didn't stop other buyers being interested in buying the property for well below market value, and taking the risk that everything would work out well for them.

The auction started and it wasn't too long before the bidding stopped at a little over $100,000. I was the highest bidder but it was still well below the banks' reserve price that they were willing to let it sell for. I'm not sure what the reserve was but it sounded like it was about $130,000 or maybe even more. This was above what I was willing to go to and so it didn't sell on the auction day. A couple of days passed and nothing had happened so I decided to increase my offer to $105,000 and see what the bank would come back with as a counter offer, if anything. Once an offer is signed, the sales-people need to call *interest* in the property and phone all the previous buyers that were keen, and any new buyers since the auction. It turned out there was another offer being drawn up as well and they of course would have known what the bidding stopped at in the auction. I decided I would go to $111,100 and if I lost out on it, I would be okay with that. Of course I had no idea what the other offer was, it could have been a lot higher than mine.

A day or so later the salesperson I was dealing with called me and said the bank had accepted my offer. I was very pleased and let the current owner living there know what had happened, and I could now keep him on as a tenant. The next step was to sign him up on a tenancy agreement which I did at $275 a week, this being slightly under market rent. I also got a registered valuation done on the property which came out at a little more than I expected at $160,000. Therefore if I had wanted to, I could have borrowed 80% of this figure being $128,000. I worked out that even if I had borrowed the full $128,000 available to me, it would have still been cash-flow positive. I didn't want to borrow any more than the $111,100 purchase price, so the extra almost $17,000 was added to the previous $15,000 extra equity credit, to now give me approximately $32,000.

Being in this position having now bought five properties in what was less than four months, I could have bought the next property at market price and still been ahead. In other words, the extra equity that had been created by buying these five properties so well, was sufficient enough to buy another rental property at market value, and still have used no equity *overall*.

PROPERTY NUMBER 5

Property Summary: -

3brm town-house, garage

Purchase price: $111,100

Rent: $275p.w.

Yield: 12.87% p.a.

Interest rate: 5.99% p.a. fixed for 18 months

Loan term: 20 years

Loan Type: P & I

Cash-flow positive/negative: $27p.w. positive

PROPERTY NUMBER 6

GEDDIS AVE, NAPIER

Another friend called me one evening in early May to let me know of a property in Napier that he knew of coming up for sale. It was a 3brm home with a single garage and also in a reasonable location, not too far away from the other two properties I had just bought in Napier. The owner apparently wanted around $125,000 which sounded fair to me. It didn't sound quite as good a deal as the previous two I had purchased there in Napier over the last month or two.

I went over and had a look at the property which was now vacant, the tenants having moved out recently. The condition was not quite as good as I had hoped it would be, needing some painting and maintenance to be done before I would be happy renting it out. It still had good potential though I thought, and after chatting for a little while we agreed on a price of $120,000 for the property as it was. After the painting and maintenance was done it would cost me $122,000 and I was thinking it should rent for $280p.w. I thought at the time that it may not quite value up to a figure to show that I was buying it at 80% of market value (would need to be $152,500). However there was more than enough equity built up in credit from the previous five properties that it shouldn't be an issue at all.

As it turned out, to my surprise the property valued to $155,000. This was higher than the Bestall St property valued to (Property Number 4), which to me was a lot better property, and I also preferred the location on that one over this one.

Sometimes valuers will take into account different things that as an investor I wouldn't consider, and the resulting figures they come up with don't seem to make any sense. Anyway it was good for me as 80% of $155,000 is $124,000 which was $2,000 more than my total cost. My equity credit therefore had now grown to $34,000 after this purchase.

PROPERTY NUMBER 6

PROPERTY SUMMARY: -

3brm home, garage

Purchase price: $120,000

Maintenance/painting: $2,000

Total Cost: $122,000

Rent: $280p.w.

Yield: 11.93% p.a.

Interest rate: 5.99% p.a. fixed for 18 months

Loan term: 20 years

Loan Type: P & I

Cash-flow positive/negative: $14p.w. positive

PROPERTY NUMBER 7

HOTENE ST, WHAKATANE

Up until 2014, I had only ever visited Whakatane once while being on holiday at nearby Ohope beach many years before that. The property I ended up buying there wasn't actually intended for me. My partner Katrina and I had been together for a little over a year at this point. She had decided shortly after I started this experiment of buying 10 properties by using no overall equity, she would like to do the same.

It was now early June 2014 and Katrina was still learning the market and going along to view properties with me when she could. It wasn't that easy as she worked from 9am until 2pm each day and then came home to see the kids after they finished school. So it was mostly in the weekends that she was able to come along with me and see the occasional property I was looking at.

A friend of mine called me from Wellington one evening and asked if I knew anything about the property market in Whakatane and I said "no not really". He was a real estate salesperson in Wellington who I'd known for more than 20 years and a client of his asked if he knew anything about the area.

I had a look on Trade Me and the prices compared to rents all seemed quite reasonable, in other words the yields looked very good. I called the salesperson for one of the properties that he listed and had a chat with him for half an hour or so. I asked him all about the area, the street this one was in, and a bit about his experience of selling properties in the area. I then called two property managers in Whakatane. One of them was managing the property that I had phoned about, and I called another company in the area to get an independent view. I asked similar questions to them both, as I had done to the salesperson. I asked how easy it was to get new tenants, what this street and area was like, general rent prices in Whakatane and how long they had been managing properties for etc. After speaking to them all for in total a bit over an hour, I thought it seemed a reasonable place to buy a rental property.

I talked to Katrina and she seemed keen to buy the one I had called up about as *her* first rental, so I called the salesperson back and talked to him more about the price. The landlord was keen to sell, having paid $130,000 for the 3brm cross-lease property about eight or nine years prior, and the property was now listed at only $105,000. It was originally listed at $119,000 a year or so earlier but had not sold, and now the vendor had dropped the price down to $105,000. The rent was $220 a week which meant close to an 11%p.a. yield already and the tenant was keen to stay on.

After a day or so we agreed on a price of $89,500 now giving the property a yield of close to 13%! Katrina had already been pre-approved to purchase her first rental property by her bank up to $130,000 and she confirmed this was still the case before she went 'cash' on the offer. Often you will get a lot better price by going cash than having conditions in your contract, but you need to have everything in order before doing this. We also arranged for a reasonably quick settlement of two or three weeks. As the tenant was staying on, the property manager didn't need to give them the 42 days notice to vacate. All was looking great. We were going to be in Rotorua the following weekend and thought we would check out the area and the property while over there. Whakatane is about an hour's drive from Rotorua, so we met the salesperson at the property, had a look through and Katrina took a whole lot of photos. It all checked out well and we were both happy with the purchase.

We got back to Hawkes Bay after the weekend, the bank already had the contract which we had emailed them the previous week and we were just waiting for the paperwork for her to sign for the mortgage. It was taking a bit longer than usual and we were wondering what the hold up with it was. Settlement was now only about a week away and still she had no mortgage documents to sign. Katrina called her bank manager again who apologised for the delay and said it should all be sorted that day. He called up later and said "sorry but we are unable to finance this property for you!" This was obviously a huge shock and she naturally asked why, to which her bank manager said it was something to do with being outside the LVR limits. This was definitely not correct. So I called him and said it was well within the LVR limits, and then he told me "well we have done some phoning around and have decided not to lend to her because of the location!" I asked him what she was supposed to do with only a week to go before settlement, and no mortgage? He said he wasn't sure but they wouldn't be able to arrange finance on the property and she would have to try somewhere else. However they would still be happy to finance any property she found up to $130,000 as long as it was anywhere in Hawkes Bay.

With only a few days before settlement I called Judy who is a mortgage broker we've put a lot of people onto in Napier. We told her what had happened and even she was amazed at what the bank had done in this case. Unfortunately the news was not good. Judy said she would need all Katrina's bank statements and lots of other information in order to get a loan approved. It could take a few days just to get an approval for a loan, and then it would take another week or so to get the documents printed and sent to her lawyer. There was now no hope of getting finance in time for her, and time was running out fast.

We talked about it and the only option was for me to settle it. Once that happened I could sell it back to her when she could arrange finance meaning extra legal costs, or for me to just keep it. I was happy to keep it and Katrina was happy for me to have it, she would keep looking for something else to buy in Hawkes Bay. As it turned out she did buy one in Flaxmere a short while later, and the loan was approved with no problems!

The Whakatane property was settled on time and all worked out fine with it in the end.

I didn't end up getting a valuation on this property, the RV or rating valuation (often called CV or GV) was $113,000 and the bank was okay to use 80% of this which is $90,400 or nearly $1,000 more than the purchase price. This again would be reflected in their calculations three months after settlement like with all the registered valuations.

PROPERTY SUMMARY: -

3brm home, off street parking

Purchase price: $89,500

Rent: $220p.w.

Yield: 12.78% p.a.

Interest rate: 5.55% p.a. fixed for 2 years

Loan term: 20 years

Loan Type: P & I

Cash-flow positive/negative: $5p.w. positive

Property Number 8

LODGE RD, NAPIER

While being away on holiday in Rotorua the weekend we looked at the Whakatane one, I had a notification that there was a new 'private sale' listed in Napier. I get the daily e-mails from Trade Me with all the new property listings in Hawkes Bay which I can access on my mobile phone.

I called the guy who owned the property and it turned out he now lived in Kawerau, not that far from Whakatane. He had previously had the property rented for a few years and now that it was vacant, he just wanted it sold.

The asking price was 'offers over $105,000' which seemed very reasonable, being a 3brm home with a garage, a sleep-out and a large section of almost 900m2. He had already had lots of calls about it and people wanting to view it.

I looked through the property on the Monday after getting back home and was keen to buy it. He was quite difficult to get in contact with, and when I did manage to talk to him, he said he already had an offer of $108,000 which he was considering taking. I said I would pay $110,000 and could settle it quickly if that helped. He said he would phone me back shortly, but a day later he still hadn't called. I phoned him again and now someone else had offered a higher price than mine and he was selling it to them instead. I asked what price they had offered him and he told me it was $111,000. I said "well, how about if I pay you $112,000 – would you sell it to me?" Again he said he would get back to me shortly! Another day went by and I hadn't heard anything back from him. So the next morning on my walk up Te Mata Peak, I phoned him and asked what was happening. Again he said someone else had now offered him $113,000! I said to him "okay, look I want to buy your property but don't want to get into an auction and not even know for sure if there really is someone else I'm bidding against". I asked him if he was serious about selling the property, and when he wanted the money by. He was genuine and said "yes I do want to sell and just want to get the best price I can". I mentioned this had already gone on for several days now and if he was keen to sell, then I was keen to buy. I said to him "tell me what price you'd be happy with, and also be able to sign a contract to sell me the property *today*?" He said "I would sell it today for $113,500". I agreed to that and then asked when he wanted settlement, and also his lawyer's details so I could draw up a contract once I got home from my walk. I would then e-mail it to his lawyer for him to sign. I drew up the contract when I got back home, then called his lawyer to say I was e-mailing it through to him. I asked him to contact his client (the vendor), and ask him to go into his office so he could sign the offer.

A day or so later I got the contract back and it was finally all done! Finance was arranged, a registered valuation was completed and the property was settled a week or so later. The valuation came back at $160,000 which was a little more than I thought it may be. At 80% of valuation, the bank would lend $128,000 on the property or $14,500 more than what I was paying for it. This meant the equity credit was now close to $50,000. The property was rented immediately for $290p.w. giving it a yield of well over 13%p.a. This easily covered all the outgoings and so strengthened my overall cash-flow position, with the eight properties I had now bought.

PROPERTY SUMMARY: -

3brm home, garage

Purchase price: $113,500

Rent: $290p.w.

Yield: 13.28% p.a.

Interest rate: 5.85% p.a. fixed for 2 years

Loan term: 20 years

Loan Type: P & I

Cash-flow positive/negative: $37p.w. positive

PROPERTY NUMBER 9

GEDDIS AVE, NAPIER

This one was another private sale, but rather than being in competition with a whole lot of other buyers like the previous purchase, the owner of this property called me. Sometimes I will run an ad in the news-paper wanting to buy properties privately. The ad will often run in the paper for three months or so with no phone calls at all. Other times I will get several calls in a month, but the owners expectations on price are way too much for me. And occasionally I will get an owner who calls me and is keen to sell, and also negotiable on price.

In this instance the landlord/owner had owned the property for six years having paid $163,000. He wanted $140,000 and being another 3brm property with a garage in an area I was beginning to know prices better, I thought it was definitely worth having a look at. I met the owner at the property an hour or so later. The tenant had recently moved out and the owner was either going to rent it out again or sell it, depending on what he could get for it. The property was on a smaller site which is often a good thing for tenants as there isn't as much lawn or gardens to look after. I was keen to buy it and the owner sounded like he wasn't really that keen on getting another tenant. The property had already dropped in value considerably since he'd purchased it, and there was no way of knowing if it would be worth even less in the future, if he had decided to hold onto it now.

Most property investors will buy property and have the assumption that prices will always go up, so will often use interest only loans, meaning the mortgage never gets paid off. If the property stays the same value for many years, or worse still – drops in value, these investors get very discouraged and can think that property investing isn't all it's made out to be. This is the time they will often get discouraged and want to sell, often for a lot less than even the current market price. I don't get concerned at all if this happens as the loan is getting paid down by the tenants over time, until there is eventually no mortgage. If the property is still worth the same money in 20 years time as when I bought it, I don't mind at all. It's of no benefit to me what I could sell it for after it's all paid off. All I want is for the property to still be a good, sound, low maintenance rental, a place where tenants like to live, and still have good cash-flow from the rent. Whether the property is worth only half the price that I paid for it, or 10 times what I paid for it, it doesn't matter to me. But what I do care about is the cash-flow that it produces. This is what separates my strategy from 95% + of the investors out there. If I had bought the property for $163,000 six years prior like this owner had done and it was worth a lot less now, it would not concern me at all, as rents do not seem to drop when prices drop. And also the mortgage is still getting paid off bit by bit every week, until it is finally all paid off.

Right now, I have a property that was purchased in 2005 to hold as a long term rental, purchase price at that time was $160,000. The market value of the property back then would have been about $170,000. I put in a 20% deposit ($32,000) and so had a loan of $128,000 which was taken out over 20 years. Over the next few years, market prices dropped at least 20 – 25% and so by 2013 it would have been worth about $130,000 or a drop of $40,000 in value. A lot of other investors were selling around this time as they had used interest only loans and now the debt on their properties was as much, and at times more than what they could sell them for.

By using a P & I loan, the mortgage on this property kept reducing and so it wasn't important to me what I could sell it for, as I didn't want to sell it! Also, what happened on this one along with many other properties I owned, the mortgages had all been fixed on four or five year interest rates. This one had been fixed for four years in 2007 at 8.9% p.a. It was at a time when all the talk was that interest rates were going to keep going up, and would soon be well over 10% p.a. The floating rates with all the banks at that time were around 10% p.a. As we all know now, interest rates didn't keep going up, they started falling drastically. A year or so later you could get a two year fixed rate loan at 6.0% p.a. and shortly after that it was even lower again. I had 15 loans locked in at interest rates of between 8.6% p.a. and 9.4% p.a. With the interest rates now at only 6.0% p.a, I was paying over $1,000 a week more in interest than I could have been paying over all these loans.

So I asked the bank that had the majority of these higher interest loans if I could pay off 5% principal on each loan. Most banks will allow you to do this annually without any penalty. This came to over $50,000 with the 10 higher interest rate loans, that I had with this particular bank. I didn't want to use my revolving credit to pay for this, so I arranged a P & I loan over five years to pay this back. Over the next two years I did the same thing again, paying down another 5% principal on these 10 loans. I did this with a four year P & I loan and lastly a three year P & I loan, at even lower interest rates again. These three short term loans are now all paid off in full.

Having paid 5% off the loan principal over three consecutive years made a big reduction in the overall *terms* of these loans. So, now in July 2106 the loan on the property mentioned above is down to only $23,000 and will be fully paid off in March 2018.

The property today is worth about $190,000. This is now more than it was 11 years ago when I purchased it, prices having moved back up significantly again in the last few years. Where the market price goes to from here on this property, or any other property, I have no idea. And as mentioned I don't mind where it goes either, as I'm only interested in what rent it brings in, not what the property may be worth. When I first bought this property in 2005, it was rented for $280p.w. Now it's rented at $300 a week, so just a small increase over that time, but more than enough to pay the small mortgage of just over $20,000 now owing on the property.

So getting back to the purchase of Property Number 9 in Napier, the vendor and I chatted for a while and agreed on a price of $130,000 which we were both happy with. I knew it would rent for $290p.w. giving me a yield of 11.6% p.a. and thought it should value to at least $155,000 when compared to the other properties I had recently purchased. As it turned out, the property only valued to $150,000. This surprised me as I had paid the most money for this one, it was the tidiest of the four Napier properties that I had recently bought, and also the one I liked the most. It may have been because the section was smaller and that had affected the value, I'm not sure, but I was happy with the purchase. At a valuation of $150,000 the bank was happy to lend 80% of this amount being $120,000. As I had paid $130,000 for this one, all it meant was that I had used $10,000 of the $50,000 equity credit (leaving $40,000) that had been built up in the previous purchases.

PROPERTY NUMBER 9

PROPERTY SUMMARY: -

3brm home, garage

Purchase price: $130,000

Rent: $290p.w.

Yield: 11.6% p.a.

Interest rate: 5.99% p.a. fixed for 18 months

Loan term: 20 years

Loan Type: P & I

Cash-flow positive/negative: $10p.w. positive

PROPERTY NUMBER 10

HOTENE ST, WHAKATANE

While we were looking at the other property that I purchased in Whakatane the weekend we were visiting Rotorua, I noticed another property that had a 'For Sale' sign on it across the road. It was a lovely looking home and also appeared to be well cared for looking at the exterior of the property, the section and the gardens. The salesperson that was showing us through the one we were looking at knew the property. His real estate company previously had it on the market for quite some time but it hadn't sold. He said it was a lovely 3brm home, well cared for and it was *owner occupied* as opposed to being a rental property. It was a 1980's home, had a double garage and was on a section size of 670m2.

I found out later when we got back to Hawkes Bay that it was on the market for $159,000 (down from $169,000 when first listed) and the current owners had paid $183,000 for it seven years earlier in 2007. I also talked to the two property managers I had talked to a week or so earlier about the other Whakatane property. I asked them their thoughts on what it would be like as a rental property and how much rent it would likely get. They both said it was a great property and would rent for $260p.w. comfortably. This all sounded great, so I called the salesperson who had the property listed and asked her all about it. She confirmed what all the others had said, it was a very nice well cared for home and priced well to sell. I asked her what price the vendors may possibly sell it for and all she said was that they had to sell it very soon. Apparently if it didn't sell soon it may go to a mortgagee sale.

With all this in mind, I thought if I could buy the property for $130,000 or maybe even slightly less it would be a great buy. The Rateable Value on the home was $149,000.

Being the last property of the 10 that I'd set out to buy over the three years, I would be well within the plan I had set out to do at the beginning of the year. It was now only June 2014 and potentially this was my 10th property already! After chatting more to the salesperson about the property, I asked her to draw up an offer of $123,000 to start with, and see what the vendors come back with. I made the contract subject to three working days finance.

A few days passed and nothing had happened so I called the salesperson. She said the vendors had seen the offer but had not made a decision on what to do yet. Another week passed by and still nothing had happened. I called the salesperson again and apparently it was now out of the vendors' hands. The contract needed to have new clauses added in to it. Even if the property sold for close to the asking price, the bank would still have to agree to the property being sold. This was because the amount owing on the mortgage would have been greater than what the vendors would have received for the property, after the agent's commission came out.

It was now July 2014 and around three weeks after putting in my offer. They had never said anything about the price even at this stage, but it was taking longer than any other contract I had ever been involved with. Another couple of days went by and nothing had happened. Then I had a call to say yet another clause had to be put in the contract, at this stage I almost withdrew the offer as it was just getting beyond ridiculous. Somehow the public trust and high court were involved as well as the bank, and it all became very confusing.

Much to my surprise the contract did eventually get signed. This happened on the 1st August, which was about six weeks after submitting my original offer. By that time the contract had been printed out so many times and emailed back and forth that it was almost illegible. However there was a long trail of emails back and forth with it, so everything was okay. Whoever was responsible for signing the contract didn't even question the price. But the offer was still subject to the bank approving the contract for a further 14 days. Luckily it only took a week for the bank to agree to this, so on the 8th August the contract was finally unconditional and I had my 10th property!

The property settled early in September 2014 and a tenant was all set to go in by this time at $260p.w. This meant the yield was 11% p.a. and I'm assuming bought about 20% below market value. I had purchased the property for $123,000 which was exactly $60,000 less than the previous owners purchased it for seven years earlier. My estimate was it was worth around $150,000 at the time, and as mentioned the RV was $149,000. I used the RV rather than getting a registered valuation, the same as I had done with the other property purchased in Whakatane.

At an RV of $149,000 the bank was okay to finance 80% of this amount, which was just over $119,000. With the purchase price of $123,000 this was

$4,000 more than the bank was prepared to lend me. This took my equity credit down from $40,000 to $36,000.

This meant I had now achieved my three year goal of buying 10 properties in only seven months (January 2014 – August 2014). I felt like it was a great achievement and wouldn't have thought it could be done in such a short time frame, when I had first started. The rents covered all the outgoings on the 20 year P & I loans, as well as the rates, the insurance and property management. Also I had not used any equity to buy these 10 properties and still had $36,000 in equity credit, meaning the overall position with my other 40 properties was even stronger than when I had started. The bank also contributed $1,000 towards each property purchase at the time of settlement. This pretty much covered most of my legal fees and the eight valuations involved in purchasing these 10 properties.

Property Summary: -

3brm home, garage

Purchase price: $123,000

Rent: $260p.w.

Yield: 10.99% p.a.

Interest rate: 5.99% p.a. fixed for 2 years

Loan term: 20 years

Loan Type: P & I

Cash-flow positive/negative: $15p.w. negative

MEETING WITH THE BANK MANAGER AGAIN - AND 10 NOW TURNS INTO 20!

At some stage in August 2014 I met up again with my bank manager Mark, and went over all the loans and finances with him. He was very pleased with how it had all worked out and very happy with the results of this experiment. Because my overall foundation and position was stronger than when I had started in January 2014, he said to me he was happy for me to buy another 10 properties if I wanted to. Up until this point I hadn't planned on buying any more than the 10 properties in the new trust, as this had been my total focus up until now. I thought about what he said and then said "yes that would be great, I would love to do another 10" as overall it had been a lot of fun doing this. He also was happy for me to buy the next 10 properties *without* getting a valuation on them, which was even better. This was because there was enough equity in all my other properties to purchase another 10 properties with 100% finance, and still be within their LVR, and interest rate cover limits.

I thought it would probably still take less than the three years in total to achieve *now buying* the 20 properties, but decided to see if I could do it all by the end of that same year! This would mean having to find another 10 property deals like the ones I had already bought, in only the next four months. If I only bought another two or three by the end of the year, it still would have been a great year for me in property.

N.B. Not only had I been buying these 10 rentals for the new trust over the last seven to eight months, I had also been buying and selling properties in my trading company. Some of these were bought and sold to other investors I know, and other properties were renovated and sold on again. I bought and sold a total of 10 properties in my trading company in 2014, making a combined profit of just over $270,000 less tax for the year.

PROPERTY NUMBER 11

ARBROATH AVE, FLAXMERE

The search was now on for another property and it was a bit like starting all over again except this time at least I knew it *could* be done. It wasn't too much longer that I bought property number 11 which was in September 2014.

It was an ex Housing New Zealand property that was put on the market to sell to first home buyers. It was a 3brm home with a new woodburner, a reasonably good size section, but no garage or carport. It was also in a street that previously had quite a poor reputation, and had now improved considerably over the last five years or so.

With Housing NZ properties, they are offered up for sale to first home buyers for three months, and if not sold after that time, they are opened up for anyone to buy. This was one that hadn't sold and was now available for other home buyers or investors to buy. It had been marketed at $115,000 and I thought it was probably worth about $125,000. I was also fairly sure it would rent for $250p.w, a little bit less than other 3brm properties I'd bought as it had no garage or carport.

After having a look through the property with the salesperson, I was happy to put in an offer. It had no oven in the kitchen which is quite common for the Housing NZ properties that go up for sale; they arrange to have a new oven installed the day, or the day before settlement. Also HNZ are generally non-negotiable with their prices so I was going to offer the full $115,000. The salesperson then called me to say there was another offer going in on the property now, so I decided to add $100 onto my price and make it a cash offer. The offer was accepted the next day so I let the bank and insurance company know when settlement was going to be.

I later found out that my friend Tom who I mentioned at the beginning of all this, had the other offer. He was the reason that triggered off this whole experiment of buying 10 properties, which had now turned into 20 properties. He had offered slightly less than me and wasn't too fussed if he bought the property or not.

The oven was installed on settlement day and I also had new curtains put up throughout the home as there was none, and also a bit of a clean on the inside.

My property manager advertised the property for rent and it took a lot longer than usual to find a tenant for this one. I wasn't sure if it was the property, or that tenant demand had slowed, or what the problem was. It also could have been that there was no garaging or carport, and also the property wasn't fenced at the time. Eventually after about three or four weeks a tenant was found. My property manager wasn't 100% sure how they would go and therefore decided to put them on a 90 day fixed term tenancy. If after 90 days everything was still good with these tenants, they would be given a *periodic tenancy* which is the standard type of tenancy used for the majority of rental properties. Katy signed the tenants up at $250p.w. which therefore gave the property a yield of 11.29% p.a.

PROPERTY SUMMARY: -

3brm home, off street parking

Purchase price: $115,100

Rent: $250p.w.

Yield: 11.29% p.a.

Interest rate: 5.99% p.a. fixed for 2 years

Loan term: 20 years

Loan Type: P & I

Cash-flow positive/negative: $3.50p.w. negative

PROPERTY NUMBER 12

FLAXMERE AVE, FLAXMERE

I had looked at this property a couple of months before purchasing it. It was originally listed for $149,000 in July 2014, so it was a possibility at the time of being one of my first 10 properties. It was now September and the property still hadn't received any offers on it. The vendors had a few properties they were selling, as they had separated, or were in the process of separating. This was making it very awkward for the company selling the property with different price expectations, amongst other things.

It was a 3brm home on a section size of over 650m2 with a single garage and the property needed a little bit of maintenance, but nothing too major. More like a bit of a tidy up really, the tenants had been there for over 15 years and wanted to stay there if possible. They were only paying $250p.w. which was at least $40 a week under the market rent. If I could buy the property for under $130,000 it would still be higher than a 10% yield with potential to increase the rent later on.

I made my offer $125,000 subject to three days finance. This is something I usually do when making an offer, make it *conditional*. I had the tenant listed on the 'sales and purchase agreement' and would keep them on as tenants if successful with buying the property. The salesperson talked to the vendors separately and both wanted more money, but didn't want to come back at a specific price. A few days went by and nothing had happened so I asked the salesperson what was happening. She said one vendor may be okay if my offer was a bit higher, but wasn't sure about the other vendor. So I asked her to increase my offer to $125,500 and make it a *cash* offer, so take out the three day finance clause. Luckily both vendors agreed to this price and each of them signed the contract over the next few days.

The yield worked out to be 10.4% p.a. which was lower than all the previous purchases, but because the tenant had been there for so many years, I decided to manage this property myself. I will occasionally do this if I think it will be an easy one to manage, and if it doesn't work out that way I will pass it on to my property manager to manage. At one time I managed all 60 - 65 properties I owned from around 2001 – 2004. Even though it was easy enough for me to do that at the time, I would not go back to managing them all myself now.

Currently in mid 2016 I own 72 properties in total and manage only nine of them. This includes two wraps (discussed in length in my 1st book) which have been going for many years now, a commercial building, a property my sister is a tenant in and five other tenancies including this one. As I was managing this one myself, I didn't mind if the yield was slightly less than all the other rental properties I had bought that year so far.

Since purchasing this property I've had the exterior painted, and also only very recently new carpet, insulation and a fence built. The rent is now $290p.w. which is still somewhat below market rent and I still manage it. If the tenant does move out at some stage, I will get the property managed and the rent will be increased to $320 - $330p.w. which would cover the property management fees.

PROPERTY SUMMARY: -

3brm home, garage

Purchase price: $125,500

Rent: $250p.w.

Yield: 10.36% p.a.

Interest rate: 5.99% p.a. fixed for 2 years

Loan term: 20 years

Loan Type: P & I

Cash-flow positive/negative: $2.50p.w. negative

PROPERTY NUMBER 13
KINGSLEY DRIVE, FLAXMERE

The same real estate company and salesperson that I purchased the previous property from also sold me this one. It was also a 3brm home with a garage and a nice section, with a tenant that had been renting there for about two years. The tenant was also keen to stay on if another investor purchased the property. The company that was selling the property was also managing it. This one was located in the same street that I'd purchased Property Number 2 in, and that one was working out very well. This one was advertised at $139,000 when it came on the market, and after talking to the salesperson for a while, I decided to offer $130,000. The tenants were paying $280p.w. which was about right, and at a purchase price of $130,000 it would make the yield 11.2% p.a.

The vendor turned down my offer initially, possibly because it had just come on the market and they thought if they held on for a while longer, they may get closer to their asking price of $139,000. The current owners had paid $158,000 for the property in 2006 and so wanted to recover some of their costs, but also knew they would already be selling at a price of $20,000 or so below what they had paid for it eight years prior to this.

A week or so went by and no other offers had come in, the salesperson then called me and said if we present the offer again and just change the settlement date slightly, they may now take my offer. We extended the settlement date out another week and also agreed to take the tenants on with the property. The vendor quickly agreed to this and signed the contract at $130,000. Sometimes it's just a matter of waiting and being patient as vendors contemplate all their options and the price being offered, especially if an offer is made when the property is first listed for sale. They will often want to see if any higher offers come in, before going back to the original one to either accept it, or negotiate. I talked to Katy my property manager after it was all signed up about taking the property over to manage from the other company, once settlement had taken place. She organised this with the existing property manager and the tenants, and it all changed over at the time of settlement a few weeks later in October 2014.

PROPERTY NUMBER 13

PROPERTY SUMMARY: -

3brm home, garage

Purchase price: $130,000

Rent: $280p.w.

Yield: 11.2% p.a.

Interest rate: 5.99% p.a. fixed for 2 years

Loan term: 20 years

Loan Type: P & I

Cash-flow positive/negative: $2.50p.w. negative

PROPERTY NUMBER 14
HUDSON RD, FLAXMERE

It wasn't too much longer before I bought the 14th property. It was around Labour weekend towards the end of October 2014. Again it was through the same company as the previous two properties I'd purchased and this property had only just been listed. It was a 3brm town-house with a single garage attached to the other town-house by the garages. The property was vacant and reasonably tidy with nothing that appeared needing to be done before it could be rented. The listing price was already fairly reasonable at $119,000 and I was fairly sure it would easily get $260 a week rent which would already make the yield well over 11% p.a. I instructed the salesperson to write up an offer for $103,000 just to see what the vendor would come back with. Like most of my offers I also made it subject to three days finance, a clause I could take out during negotiations to make the offer more attractive if needed.

Being Labour weekend in Hawkes Bay, the Friday here is also HB anniversary day, a public holiday when most people go to the local show. The offer had been submitted the day before and the vendor was now going into the real estate office in Hastings on the Friday morning, to consider the offer. The salesperson I was dealing with was away for the long weekend and normally what happens is *that* person will be the only one that communicates with me, being the buyer. In this case she was out of town for the weekend so I asked her to see if it would be okay for me to go into the office as well and wait in another room. I knew the listing salesperson for the property as well, so rather than wait until after the long weekend to see my salesperson again, I asked if it would be okay for me to negotiate the offer with the listing salesperson instead. If it all went through okay, my salesperson would still get her commission for selling the property. They were both happy with that, so I went to the office about 10 minutes after the vendors were meeting with the listing salesperson.

Another 10 minutes went by and then the salesperson came in to see me with a counter-signed offer. The vendors had come back at $110,000 which was a very good price I thought. I went back immediately with $105,500 still with the three day finance clause in the contract. I sat there for 15 minutes or so and the salesperson then came back in and said "no that's it, $110,000 is as low as they will go. The property was only listed a couple of days ago and nobody else has seen it yet. They will wait it out and see if they can get the

$110,000 they want". I said to him "okay let's make it cash now at the same price of $105,500 and just see what they come back with. Even if it's just a little bit under $110,000 just see what you can do. Being a cash offer, they can go away and enjoy the weekend knowing that it's sold". So he went back and chatted to them for another 15 minutes or so, and came back into see me. They had agreed to come down to $109,000 and that was it, not a cent less. I was very happy with that and agreed immediately, so I signed the contract at that price and it was all done.

It was a great experience doing the negotiations that way in the office with myself, the vendor, and the salesperson all there at the same time. It could have saved us all several days of going back and forth between four of us, and then another buyer could have come into it, and then I would have possibly been competing with them as well. That's one of the main reasons I prefer to buy houses privately, you can usually get a deal done a lot faster. Also you usually get a good feel as to how negotiable the vendor is. It's often very difficult to know what's really happening when dealing through an agent, difficult in that you have a third and often a fourth party involved in the negotiations as well.

With this property I was able to get my property manager Katy through the following week to take some photos and advertise it for rent. She believed it would rent for $265 a week being so nice and tidy, and within a week or two she had someone suitable for it. The property settled shortly thereafter and the new tenant moved in. Being able to purchase the property for $10,000 less than the asking price, as well as getting more rent than I had initially planned on, meant that the yield rather than being just over 11% was now 12.64%. This made it now one of the highest yielding properties purchased so far during the year. Little did I know then that my next purchase would have an even higher yield, and turn out to be my best purchase of the year!

PROPERTY NUMBER 14 SUMMARY: -

3brm town-house, garage

Purchase price: $109,000

Rent: $265p.w.

Yield: 12.64% p.a.

Interest rate: 5.75% p.a. fixed for 2 years

Loan term: 20 years

Loan Type: P & I

Cash-flow positive/negative: $24p.w. positive

PROPERTY NUMBER 15

DUNDEE DRIVE, FLAXMERE

Every Wednesday a couple of good friends of mine Jim and Andrew who are also property investors have lunch together somewhere in Hastings. We catch up for a chat mostly about property and talk about what we've all been up to for the week. I also have lunch once a month with the local real estate salespeople that I mostly deal with, Jason and David from Property Brokers. Over the last 10 years they would have been involved in at least 100 transactions, either with me buying through them or selling through them. Previously to that I used to buy and sell through Paul, Jason's older brother for five years or so, starting in the year 2000. I would have done close to 100 transactions with Paul as well. Jason took over his business when Paul became the sales manager. On this occasion one day in late October 2014, I was having lunch with my property managers Katy and Jamie from Oxygen. Katy is such an amazing property manager and manages most of my properties in Hastings. We talk pretty much every day about something happening with one of the 50 or so properties she manages. Jamie is great as well; she mostly does the letting of all the properties, i.e. finding suitable tenants when properties become vacant. The two of them make life as a landlord for me so much easier, always keeping me informed of what's going on with any vacancies, re-letting, or maintenance on any of the properties, and are the best property managers I could have ever wished for.

It was almost time to finish up at lunch when Katy mentioned to me that one of her landlords may be keen to sell their property in Flaxmere. It had quite a few dampness issues, had been difficult to tenant in the last few years and was in major need of a complete overhaul. Previously the property had 11 people living in it and had mould on the walls and the ceilings. It really needed to be renovated as well as the dampness issues being all sorted, before putting in another tenant. I had a look at it later that day and I don't think many people would have wanted to live there, it was in a really bad state and in need of some serious work. The landlord had owned the property for eight years and paid $175,000 for it. The price she paid back then would have been top dollar for it, even if it was immaculate. Not surprising to me was the valuation on the property I looked at, which was done when the current owner had purchased it, saying it was worth $175,000.

N.B. I say not surprising because valuations can be all over the place and I don't put much significance on them at all. The banks want them for an indication of value for financing purposes which is fair enough. But with the huge variance I've seen in several cases with two valuers doing registered valuations on the same property in the same week, I don't rely on them as being that accurate at all. The only real way is to know the market prices well yourself, which does take time.

In its current condition and comparing it to other recent purchases, I didn't think it was worth me paying much more than $100,000 for it. The property did have great potential though, being a 3brm home with a double garage on a 650 m2 section, and the street was also very good. After looking through the property I said to Katy that it's going to need a lot of work. Inside needed a complete clean and paint, there were also holes in some of the walls that would need repairing and plastering. The bath needed replacing as did the bathroom vanity unit, and the kitchen really needed pulling out completely, and starting again. Some of the exterior weatherboards were rotting and the more I looked the more I found needed doing. I realised after a while that the exterior was actually clad in weatherside, not something I had seen on a property for quite some time. It was a product that had stopped being produced in the late 1970's or early 1980's because of the way it reacts to water. If the boards are kept well maintained and painted, there should never be an issue with it. But when exposed to water it goes like weetbix and will crumble just by rubbing it between your fingers. With this cladding it needs to be regularly inspected for any paint chips as any moisture on the boards can damage them fairly quickly. Quite a few properties around the district still have this cladding on, and look as good as new. Fair Go had run a programme in the 1980's about this and the owners who had this type of cladding were all offered $5,000 to replace the weatherside cladding. A lot of properties were done and there were also a lot that weren't done for one reason or another. Whether the owners didn't know or hadn't seen the programme on Fair Go I'm not sure. As far as I remember though, it actually came up again in an episode a few years later and the same $5,000 offer was given again as many owners hadn't known about it. That was well over 30 years ago now, but there are still quite a few properties around with this cladding.

At the time of looking at the property I was 95% sure it was weatherside cladding and after looking through the previous valuation report in more detail, it confirmed it.

Katy thought the owner wanted around $115,000 for it but wasn't sure. She called her up while I was there and asked how much she wanted for the property. It was around that figure but was very keen to sell it. I had told Katy that if the cladding had been something else or at least was in good order, I would be prepared to pay around $105,000 - $110,000. After phoning and talking to a couple of builders while still on-site, they said it could be anywhere from $15,000 - $20,000 to replace the boards, and then it also needed to be painted. It was all sounding very expensive to me, so I had to take that into account with how much I would be willing to pay for the property.

After some time we agreed on a price of $88,500. I still had a few doubts about how much it was all going to cost, not ever having reclad a property like this previously.

The contract was all signed and with the property being vacant, I had asked if it was possible to start doing some of the work on it prior to settlement. The vendor agreed and so this was written into the contract. Settlement was to take place around six weeks later, being the 1st week of December 2014.

Work was started a few days later with cleaning the ceilings and walls, plastering and painting. The bathtub was taken out and another good 2nd hand one was put in with a frame having to be built around it, and new seratone on the walls. The builder also put in a good 2nd hand vanity unit and kitchen. Another builder did the exterior, replacing the weatherside cladding. He also insulated inside the walls as he replaced all the boards. Once finished the exterior was painted and new carpet and vinyl was put down inside. The home already had a fairly new woodburner that had been installed, which I think may have been put in to attempt to solve the dampness issues inside the property.

Within four or five weeks the renovation was all finished and it came in well under budget which is quite rare. I had allowed around $30,000 - $35,000 for everything to be done and it ended up costing only $22,000 which was a bonus. The exterior was totally reclad for only $10,000 and all the interior painting and plastering, as well as the exterior painting was done by someone that had wanted to rent the property once it had been renovated.

The guy and his family wanted a good job done before they moved in, so said they would like to do all the plastering and painting themselves. They could also do it for a lot less than any other painter and plasterer would do it for. I agreed and they did do a great job. I had told them before the start of the renovations that they could rent the property for $300p.w. which they were very happy with. Once it was all complete though, they told me only a few days before they were due to move in, that they'd been accepted for a new home grant. They were going to be buying their own property only a few houses away from this one. I let Katy know after they told me they wouldn't be moving in now, and within a few days she had new tenants lined up ready to go in at $320p.w.

Settlement took place in early December 2014 and the new tenants moved in about a week or so after that.

All up the property had cost me $88,500 to purchase it, plus $22,000 for all the renovations. In total $110,500. I estimated the value of the property to be somewhere around $150,000 - $155,000 after all the renovation work was completed. At $150,000 an 80% mortgage on this amount would be $120,000. With this purchase, it's the only property I ended up borrowing *more* than the total cost of the property after the renovation work. I did this because even by borrowing $10,000 more than my overall costs, it was still only 80% of the value of what I believed the property to be worth.

As mentioned earlier on, the bank was fine with me not having to get registered valuations on all these properties after the first 10 were purchased. In this instance though I decided to get a registered valuation done because, on their books, it would show a purchase price of $88,500 and lending 80% on that amount is only $70,800. This means that it would have taken about $40,000 of *perceived* equity away from my existing properties in the eyes of the bank ($110,500 total costs after reno minus a bank loan of $70,800). Because of this I went ahead and got a registered valuation done on the property, and it came back to me a couple of days later saying it was worth $170,000. So I *could have* borrowed 80% of this 'registered valuation' figure being $136,000. But as mentioned I decided to only borrow $120,000 which was still nearly $10,000 *more* than my *total* costs. In effect what this meant was that I bought the property, renovated it, and then received $10,000 back *more* than my total costs of buying and renovating the property. The rent of $320p.w. would easily cover the mortgage of $120,000 and because my overall costs were only $110,500, the yield was in reality a little over 15% p.a.

In the summary below the yield and cash-flow is shown as *less* than what it would have been if I'd borrowed $110,500 from the bank, *rather* than the $120,000 that I did borrow.

PROPERTY NUMBER 15 SUMMARY: -

3brm home, garage

Purchase price: $88,500

Renovation costs: $22,000

Total costs: $110,500

Mortgage: $120,000

Rent: $320p.w.

Yield: 13.87% p.a. (*Yield on $110,500 - after reno costs: 15.05%p.a.)*

Interest rate: 5.75% p.a. fixed for 2 years

Loan term: 20 years

Loan Type: P & I

Cash-flow positive/negative: $55p.w. positive

PROPERTY NUMBER 16

HOOD ST, HASTINGS

While all the renovation work had been going on with the previous property purchase, I was still out looking for other properties to buy. One thing I learned many years ago is the value of my *time*. As mentioned briefly in my 1st book in 2003 and the update in 2008, I renovated a couple of properties in Dannevirke while living there almost 20 years ago, back in the late 1990's. I spent many hours painting, sanding exteriors, mowing lawns, taking away rubbish and all sorts of things renovating two properties over a period of six months or so. We also had trades-people do all the building, plumbing and electrical work to the properties as well as carpet and vinyl laid in both properties. What I realised though is that I was paying tradespeople $30 an hour and I was basically working for the same money. I could have paid someone else $30 an hour to do what I was doing, and been out looking for other properties to buy. It took me that long to realise the importance of my time and *how much* my time was worth. Rather than sanding weatherboards or painting, I could have been out looking for another property to buy. From memory there was a profit of $15,000 or so after expenses on each property, which at the time was a reasonable amount, considering the first of the two properties only cost $16,000!

With the renovation projects I do now, the profit usually works out to be around $30,000 after all expenses before tax. If I was still doing some of the work myself I would be saving $30 - $50 an hour, but costing me my *time,* which is a lot more valuable. Some renovation projects take very little time to organise all the tradespeople to do the work, and some take a lot longer, but it's still far less time involved than *me* doing all the work myself. It's more of a mindset than anything. If you really believe your time is worth say $500+ per hour, you will be reluctant to do anything for less than that. That is, unless you are doing someone else a favour, contributing in some way or because you choose to do it.

So with the previous property that was purchased above and renovated, if I'd decided to paint it myself to save money by paying someone else, I would have cost myself the *next* six property deals that were bought by the time Property Number 15 was settled. Those six properties over time would be worth $800,000 or more to me, plus the ongoing cash-flow of $6,000 a month after they're all paid off. Many people think they are saving money by doing all the work themselves, but actually it could be costing them far more money in *lost* opportunities.

It's not true in all cases, you may only have the funding to do one property at a time and not be able to purchase anything more until a project is finished and sold again. However it's important to keep thinking to yourself, am I using my time wisely, or could I be paying someone else to do what I'm doing? What dollar figure per hour do you put on your own time, and what are your highest 'dollar per hour' activities? For me, it's finding a property and negotiating a good deal on it.

Over the last three years or so I've completed more than 75 property purchases including the 20 buy and hold properties mentioned here in this experiment. Some of the 55 properties (not relating to the experiment) were also held as rentals and put into my original buy and hold trust. One of my most recent goals in property was to have 60 long term buy and holds, 40 in my original trust and 20 in the new trust. Of these 55 properties purchased, 13 of these were bought as rentals for long term buy and holds, and the other 42 were traded/renovated and sold on again. Some of these trades needed very little work done before they were sold on again, and others were bigger renovation projects that took from a few weeks up to a few months to complete.

The point I'm really wanting to make is that most of these deals wouldn't have happened had I been trying to save money by doing all the painting myself, mowing lawns, or working for someone else and being paid $25 - $30 per hour. The last paid job I had working for wages was when I was age 26 and worked as a mechanic for $15 per hour. If I hadn't decided to stop trading *hours* for *dollars* back then, I may still have been working as a mechanic. I loved the job, the people, and the work I was doing. But not enough to make me want to keep doing it for another 40 years, and have a high probability of ending up with very little or nothing, at the end of it. There's such a sense of freedom not having to drive to work in traffic five or six days a week. Also, not having to be at a job at a certain time every day, told how many hours to work, how much they will give me for a week's work, told when I can have a lunch or a tea break, told when to go home, and then only allowed to have a few weeks off every year for a holiday. Doing that for 45 years or more and ending up broke, and then having to *rely* on a pension, isn't my idea of a life of freedom, fun and doing all the things I want to in life. Obviously there's a need for people to be employed. Not many people can go tell their boss they aren't coming back to work anymore because it's not that much fun being told what to do all the time, and they're not being paid enough.

What I'm saying is that there is a need for people to be working, to be employed and feel like they have the security of a pay-cheque every week that they can rely on. That will probably not change in my lifetime or yours. What I am saying is that it's a choice and if you don't enjoy your job, and want something more out of life, there may be a way for you. Especially if you have a *big enough* 'why' and are determined to do all you can to go for what it is you *really* want. It may not be in property, it may mean owning your own business, or going into an area of work that makes better use of your talents or your strengths, and doing more of the things you love to do. I just don't see the point in working for wages for your entire lifetime when you really don't enjoy what you're doing. The statistics show that over 80% of people don't like their job and only 13% of people really love what they do.

Now moving onto Property Number 16, this one was another one that was purchased through the same salesperson as three of the previous four properties and was a relatively easy one. It was a very tidy 1950's 3brm home in Hastings on a large 850m2 section, and also had a single garage. The street it's located in isn't one I would have considered owning a rental in a few years ago. The street though has improved a lot over time and I thought it would be fine to buy in now, as long as the numbers worked out okay.

The current owners had been there for many years and were keen to sell and move on. The property had already been on the market for a couple of months and had recently been reduced down to an asking price of $159,000. It was a fairly easy and quick negotiation on this one and we soon agreed on a price of $150,000. The property was settled a few weeks later and a tenant was found by my property manager Katy a couple of weeks later for $300p.w. This gave the property a 10.4% p.a. yield.

Property Number 16 Summary: -

3brm home, garage

Purchase price: $150,000

Rent: $300p.w.

Yield: 10.4% p.a.

Interest rate: 5.75% p.a. fixed for 2 years

Loan term: 20 years

Loan Type: P & I

Cash-flow positive/negative: $14p.w. negative

PROPERTY NUMBER 17
CAERNARVON DR, FLAXMERE

A good friend of mine had mentioned this property to me several months earlier. It was a friend of hers who was looking at selling her home and moving over to Napier to be closer to her business and where she worked. She had bought the property 11 years earlier and paid a little over $80,000 for it at that time. It was a 1970's 3brm home with a carport, on a section size of 670m2. The floor area was 120m2 which is quite large for a standard 3brm home in Flaxmere, and was in really tidy condition. At the time that my friend had told me to call the owner, I went over to have a chat with her and have a look through the property. We talked a little bit about price and were fairly close on our thinking with that, but she wasn't quite ready to sell and make the move at that time. I followed her up with a phone call a couple of times after that and now in early November she was ready to look at moving.

If you are buying privately and don't agree to purchase the property at the time when you first view it, it's very important to follow up every now and then, just to see how they are getting on. Sometimes it's not the right time for the owner to move and sometimes their expectations on price may not be quite the same as what you're willing to pay. If there's virtually no chance of an agreement being made now or in the foreseeable future, then there isn't really much point in following up further with it. Many times I've kept in communication every month or so for six months and longer with a private seller, and then bought the property from them. Often it's just a quick call to see how they're going if they have it on the market themselves; or if they've had any more thoughts on selling it now, if they hadn't been quite ready at the time when first viewing it.

N.B. One property I purchased earlier this year (2016) was advertised on Trade Me for $189,000 and needed quite a lot of renovation work and wasn't worth anywhere near that much in my opinion. It was another property with weatherside cladding which had quite a few flaking boards but the rest were in 'as new' condition. Inside needed painting, new carpet and vinyl, quite *a bit of electrical work and it also needed a new woodburner. I estimated it would cost about $20,000 for me to renovate it, and then be worth around $190,000 - $195,000 after the renovation work. For it to work for me I would need to buy the property for less than $150,000 and preferably around $140,000. If I had paid $150,000 spent $20,000 on renovations and then sold it for $190,000; after holding costs, legal fees and agent's commission there would be very little left. It would have been perfect as a rental property at the right price once renovated, but by this time I wasn't looking at purchasing any more buy and holds. I must have talked to, or texted the owner at least 10 – 15 times over the next few months to see how she was getting on. Nobody was prepared to pay her anything close to what she was asking for the property, but eventually she said she would take $150,000. This was less than what she originally paid for the property, more than 10 years earlier. It was still very marginal at that price if I was to renovate it and sell it on again, but at least now it was a lot closer to what I thought it was worth. A few other investors I know had also looked at the property and had thought it was worth around the same money as what I was thinking.*

Eventually three to four months after contacting the owner, we finally agreed on a price of $143,000 with vacant possession. I found out after the contract was all signed and gone unconditional, a couple of other investors had been very close to doing a deal with her as well, but were slightly less than me with their offers.

Before doing any work to the property, I offered it to four other investors I know well who were looking at rental properties to buy. I would settle it and then they could buy it off me for another $6,000 more than what I had paid, and it should be a very good rental property for them after that. It was in one of the best streets in Flaxmere and would be easy to get a good tenant in. I thought at the time the margins were still going to be quite small for me and for all the work of organising tradespeople to do the work etc, I may only make $10,000 - 15,000 or so after all expenses on the deal. So if I could sell it for a profit of $5,000 (after legal fees) without doing any work to it, it would be worth it for me. All four investors turned it down and said no thanks, they didn't want it.

I settled on the property a couple of weeks later and started organising the work to be done. The rotten boards were all replaced; the whole exterior of the home and also the garage was painted in a nice modern light grey colour with darker base boards, and the same darker grey under the windows. It had been a light green colour previously and painting it in the new grey colour that my partner Katrina said would look great, had really made a big difference to the appearance of the property. Around the exterior, the grounds were tidied up, some trees trimmed or removed, and some minor repairs to the fence. The interior work was carried out including painting, electrical work, new curtains, a new woodburner, insulation, and also a good 2nd hand laundry washtub that was given to me by someone in the free 12 month mentoring group, was also put in.

About three weeks later the renovation work was all complete and the property had come up a lot better than I had imagined. I asked Jason and David the salespeople I usually use to sell properties, to come and have a look and get their thoughts on what it might be worth now. They suggested listing it with a price of 'offers over $195,000'. The renovation work was a little less than I had originally budgeted on, costing me $17,000 in total. This meant the after reno costs were a total of $160,000. Had I bought the property to renovate and keep it as a rental, it would have been a great property for this. I knew it would now rent for $320 giving the property a yield of 10.4% p.a. Now in 2016 properties are about 20% higher than price they were when I was buying the 20 properties to hold in 2014. Rents have only increased marginally so overall the yields are a lot less than they were in 2014. A 10% yield now is almost impossible to get, but with interest rates almost 2% p.a. less than they were in 2014, the cash-flow works out very similar. Here is what this property would have looked like had I been buying it to hold: -

FEBRUARY 2016 RENOVATION PROPERTY SUMMARY, IF PURCHASED AS A RENTAL: -

3brm home, garage
Purchase price: $143,000
Renovation cost: $17,000
Total cost: $160,000
Rent: $320p.w.

PROPERTY NUMBER 17

Yield: 10.4% p.a.
Interest rate: 4.2% p.a. fixed for 2 years
Loan term: 20 years
Loan Type: P & I
Cash-flow positive/negative: $21p.w. positive

You can see even though the yield of 10.4% p.a. is exactly the same as the

Before reno

After reno

previous property purchased (number 16), the cash-flow rather than being $14p.w. negative is now $21p.w. positive. That's the difference the interest rate makes, 1.5%p.a. less now than it was two years ago in 2014. People will often say to me you can't get the yields now that I was getting in 2014 and I tell them the overall cash-flow is very similar now on a 9% yield than it was then having an 11% p.a. yield with the higher interest rates.

As mentioned earlier this property wasn't bought as a buy and hold, and was therefore purchased in my trading company. If Jason and David could sell the property for $195,000 there was a very good profit now of $35,000 less their commission, GST, income tax and a small amount for holding costs. At the time it was listed we were due to go on another cruise out of Sydney, this one was for eight nights up the coast to Brisbane and Airlee Beach. With very little mobile coverage being out at sea for most of the trip, we organised a deadline sale for two weeks after listing the property, and hopefully by the time we got back from our trip there may be an offer. We got back, and on the Monday evening Jason and David came around home and had two offers on the property. Because there were two offers, both buyers knew they were in competition with someone else and had to put their best offer in. This has been happening with a lot of sales this year as there are a lot of buyers wanting properties and not a lot of listings around. The highest offer was $205,100 so $10,100 more than the asking price. I signed it and within a week or so the contract was unconditional. This meant a profit of around $35,000 after the agent's commission, and before tax and holding/legal costs. It ended up being a very worthwhile trade and worked out better than I originally thought. I was therefore quite pleased that none of the four investors I had previously offered the property to, had bought it!

Going back now to 2014 and the private sale I was working on, we quickly agreed on a price of $138,500 and I thought at the time the property would rent for about $280 - $290 as it had no garaging, only the carport.

A couple of weeks later the property settled and part of the agreement was the owner would stay on at a slightly reduced rent until she moved over to Napier. It turned out she was only there a week or so and then gave me notice that she was going to be moving in three weeks time. So my property manager Katy advertised the property for rent and a tenant was soon found for a rent of $300p.w. which was better than I had expected. Nothing needed to be done to the property and the tenant moved in shortly thereafter.

PROPERTY NUMBER 17 SUMMARY: -

3brm home, carport

Purchase price: $138,500

Rent: $300p.w.

Yield: 11.2% p.a.

Interest rate: 5.55% p.a. fixed for 2 years

Loan term: 20 years

Loan Type: P & I

Cash-flow positive/negative: $10p.w. positive

PROPERTY NUMBER 18
SCOTT DR, FLAXMERE

Before getting into the purchase of this property, I want to talk a bit about yields and the way to look at these, long term. You may have heard before that it's best to constantly review the yields on your properties and if they get too low, then you should sell these properties and buy higher yielding ones. Accountants often recommend this to property investors and a very well known overseas investor and author was also a big promoter of this, he used to be an accountant before becoming a full time investor.

To give you a couple of examples of what I mean, let's say you purchased a property 10 years ago for $150,000 and at the time the property was rented for $280p.w. This would give you a yield of 9.71% p.a. ($280 x 52 weeks/$150,000). Now 10 years later the property is worth $280,000 and is rented for $320p.w.

The accountant and many investors would now say that your yield is less than it was when you purchased it; and if you work out it, is now only 5.94% p.a. This compares to a yield of 9.71% p.a. when you purchased it ($320 x 52 weeks/$280,000).

And let's say another property was purchased 15 years ago for $240,000 and was at that time rented for $340p.w. giving a yield of 7.37% p.a. ($340 x 52 weeks/$240,000). Today the property has risen in value and is now worth $600,000 but the rent has only gone up to $420p.w. Many accountants would say your yield is now only 3.64% p.a. ($420 x 52 weeks/$600,000). They may say to you that your yield has halved compared to when you bought it. It's now only returning you the same interest as you would be getting if your money was in the bank, and is less than the interest rate you are paying on your mortgage. They may also suggest to you to sell these properties and buy some higher yielding ones which will make more sense. While I can see some logic to this, there is a problem with it. In order to find higher yielding properties to match what you had at the time of purchasing these two properties, you will most likely have to buy in a far less desirable location. You would be extremely unlikely to be able to purchase two properties in a similar location to these two properties that you purchased many years ago that would now give you 9.7% p.a. as in the first example and 7.37% p.a. in the second example. This is of course because not only did your properties go up in value, but so did everybody else's! The only way now to get a better yield in the same city is to buy in a not so good area where you will get a higher yield, but also a less desirable neighbourhood.

In Hawkes Bay where I live, house prices now range from around $160,000 for a standard 3brm home up to around $350,000. The only difference is the location of these properties. The properties could be identical, but because of the location they're in, one property is worth more than twice as much as the other one. That would be the same for almost any city in NZ with a population of 100,000 + people. You have great locations and very safe, secure neighbourhoods and some streets where you may not want to walk down alone after 10p.m.

So for me, the yield is only important when you *buy* the property, not in several years time when prices may have gone up a lot, and rents have only increased slightly. There are times when you buy a property to hold as a rental and either it's under rented, or the property may need some renovation work to be carried out before being able to get market rent. In these cases you want to work out what the yield is going to be *after* the rent is brought back up to the current market rate, or the renovation work is completed, so you can now achieve a higher rent. The renovation work of course is added to your purchase price and then you work out the yield by determining what the new rent will be. As an example, let's say you purchase a property for $140,000 that needs work and because of this, is rented at only $240p.w. The current yield is therefore 8.91%p.a. You now spend $15,000 on some much needed repairs and maintenance and are now able to rent the property out for $310p.w. Your total spend is therefore $155,000 and with the property now rented at $310p.w. the yield works out to be 10.4%p.a. ($310 x 52 weeks/$155,000). So work out the yield at the time you buy if the rent is already at market rate, or the all up costs after any maintenance and repair costs are completed, and what the new rent will be.

This now brings me to Property Number 18. In 2006, eight years before I bought this property, it was purchased for $195,000. From 2005 to 2014 rents changed very little in Hawkes Bay, so I imagine it would have rented at a similar amount in 2006. The rent was $285p.w. when I purchased the property in late 2014. If the rent was say $285p.w. in 2006 when the previous owner bought the property, the yield at that time would have been 7.6%p.a. which was an okay yield. At that time, I was looking for properties with yields of over 8%p.a. so it wasn't too far off that. With the GFC (global financial crisis) affecting property prices in Hawkes Bay from 2007 for a number of years, prices in the region here dropped slowly over that time, in some cases dropping by 20 – 30% from their highs.

The vendor of this property had listed it for sale with an agent in February 2014 for $180,000 and it had sat on the market for nine months and still hadn't sold. I bought the property in November 2014 for $144,000 which I think was good value for what it was. It was a very tidy 3brm home with garage on a section size of over 800m2, and I estimated the market value to have been around $160,000 - $165,000. I had got a very good deal buying it because the vendor now 'just wanted it sold'. It had sat on the market for a very long time, and maybe the vendor's expectations were too high when it was first listed. Some of the salespeople may have believed the price was unrealistic and their buyers may also have been put off by the high asking price. It's hard to say, but often when a property is listed at too high a price to begin with, it ends up selling for a lot less than it would have, had it been priced correctly to begin with.

A lot of the properties that I purchased in 2012 – 2015 were bought from investors who now had little or no equity in their properties because of the market values dropping so much. As mentioned earlier, a lot of investors only buy a property because they think it will *always* go up in value. They generally use interest only loans as they think 'why pay off the debt if the price is going to double in 10 years time?' Many say 'I will just buy 10 properties and in 10 years time they will have all doubled in value, so I'll sell five of them then and pay off the debt on the other five properties. That will give me five good properties with no debt and a good income'. That's how a lot of investors still think today. There are a couple of problems with that; firstly prices don't always do what you hope or think they will do, and secondly if they do double in value – they don't sell half of them to pay off the debt on the others. What generally happens is they think they are smart and because they were right about prices doubling, they think it will happen again and again, continuously. So now they want to borrow more money and buy more properties with all the extra equity they have. They go out and buy another 5 – 10 properties and expect prices to double again. This may go on for some time and all the while they are highly leveraged because of all the extra debt they have created, by buying so many more properties (anything over a 70% LVR I think is high when you have over $2 million borrowed). When the properties these people buy don't behave in a way they think they should, they blame the location where they bought, or simply think property investing isn't all it's made out to be, or is too risky and decide to sell their properties. It's not that property investing is necessarily risky, it's that the *investor* themselves is the risk. They start investing with certain assumptions and when these assumptions don't happen, they lay the blame on something *other* than themselves.

To show you how this works; with Property Number 18 here that I purchased, let's assume the previous owner put in a 20% deposit of $39,000 on their $195,000 purchase price. The mortgage would therefore have been $156,000 in 2006 and most likely was an interest only loan. At the time interest rates for mortgages were around 8 – 9%p.a. An interest only loan of $156,000 at 8.0% p.a. is $240p.w. If you add on the rates and insurance of around $45p.w, it would have been fairly much break even if the rent was $285p.w. at the time.

Now eight years later, the debt is still $156,000 and the property is worth considerably less than what they paid for it. This may have been the reason why the property was first listed at such a high price compared to what it was now worth. As mentioned, the list price in early 2014 was $180,000 and from memory it had come down to an asking price of $159,000 when I looked at it. If the mortgage was still $156,000, they would lose all of their $39,000 deposit plus have to put in more money just to sell it when you take off the agent's sales commission. At this point many investors will seriously just want to sell and wish the problem would go away. They may be thinking 'I paid $195,000 for this property eight years ago and now it's only worth $150,000 and I still owe $156,000 on the mortgage! What will it be worth in another eight years time, maybe even less again?'

It wouldn't be a nice situation to be in, and if they had bought the property with less *assumptions* and more *thought* to begin with, it could have all worked out well for them. Today the property is worth around $190,000 again, very close to what they originally paid for it. But with me eventually buying the property for $144,000 nine months after it was originally listed; my yield was a very reasonable 10.29%p.a.

I wonder if the same accountants mentioned earlier that recommend investors to sell their investment properties when it appears their yields have gone down over time, would now have recommended this owner to have kept this property, as his yield was *now a lot higher* than when he purchased the property! ☺ Somehow I don't think so, and you can hopefully now see the logic of why I'm only interested in the yields of investment properties when buying them, not what they may *appear to be* years later.

PROPERTY NUMBER 18 SUMMARY: -

3brm home, garage

Purchase price: $144,000

Rent: $285p.w.

Yield: 10.29% p.a.

Interest rate: 5.55% p.a. fixed for 2 years

Loan term: 20 years

Loan Type: P & I

Cash-flow positive/negative: $12p.w. negative

PROPERTY NUMBER 19

SHACKLETON ST, NAPIER

It was November 2014, and now it was looking like I may actually be able to get to my goal of buying 20 properties in just one year. What had started out as a goal of buying 10 properties within three years using no equity, changed after reaching that goal in only seven months. December is a bit of a strange month with real estate as most people are looking forward to Christmas, holidays, and time off. It's not usually as good a time to be looking for, or buying properties, with so many people rushing about. However, after purchasing the previous property in mid November, I only needed two more properties and the target would be reached.

This turned out to be a very easy one in the end, another friend called me about a property in Napier where the owner was keen to sell and settle before Christmas. It was a lovely 1950's 3brm home on a 700m2 section in a good street and with an existing tenant wanting to stay. The owner wanted a very reasonable $130,000 for it if the settlement could happen fairly quickly, the tenant was paying $280p.w. It was a property where again the owner had bought the property several years earlier for a lot more money. The property had been purchased as an investment in late 2005 for $173,000 and is another example of a property being sold nearly 10 years later for around 25% less than what the owner had paid for it. Now only two years later, the property is worth about $185,000 - $190,000 and I estimated it was worth about $150,000 at the time I looked at it.

The price was fine and so I didn't negotiate, it was worth paying the $130,000 to me, the only thing I would need to do is put in a heat pump as it had no heating. I agreed to buy the property, and the sales and purchase agreement was completed with settlement to be a few weeks later.

The change over and settlement all went well so now I only wanted one more property to reach my target of 20 rental properties for the year.

PROPERTY NUMBER 19 SUMMARY: -

3brm home, carport

Purchase price: $130,000

Heat pump: $2,000

Total Cost: $132,000

Rent: $280p.w.

Yield: 11.03% p.a.

Interest rate: 5.55% p.a. fixed for 2 years

Loan term: 20 years

Loan Type: P & I

Cash-flow positive/negative: $5p.w. positive

PROPERTY NUMBER 20
WEDDELL ST, FLAXMERE

Only a few days later, my daily Trade Me e-mail with the new properties that had just listed, came through to me. One of the new listings was a private sale that had been on with a couple of agents during the year but had not sold. At the beginning of the year it had been listed for about $175,000 and sat on the market for several months. Then it was listed with another agent in town for $159,000 and was withdrawn several months later when again it did not sell. It was now vacant and the owner wanted it sold. From memory he had paid over $170,000 for it several years earlier and now needed close to $140,000 to clear the mortgage and come out with nothing. It is yet another example of investors buying properties with assumptions, and not having a good safe strategy that works in any market – up, down or sideways.

N.B. In the 'Property Number 9' summary you may recall the property I bought in 2005 for $160,000 in Flaxmere and in 2013 it was worth only about $130,000. For me I really didn't even consider it to be a bad thing that it was now worth a lot less than I had paid for it, as the debt on it was rapidly reducing, and would all be paid off within a few years. But if I had made the assumption that prices always go up and therefore used an interest only loan, my debt would have been equal to what the property was worth. As mentioned, prices have increased again to what they had been at their highs in 2006 – 2007 and now are even higher again. To me, this isn't such a good thing as it has made the yields a lot lower for new investors wanting to get into the market. However, as mentioned previously with interest rates now lower in 2016 than they were in 2013 – 2014, it hasn't made much of a difference with the <u>overall</u> cash-flow.

The vendor of this one was advertising the property on Trade Me for $145,000 which showed to me he was serious about selling. I called him and had a good long chat to him about the property and what his situation was. It was a tidy 3brm home with a garage on a 700m2 section in a reasonable location in Flaxmere. It was in a street I had not ever looked at properties in previously, nor had even driven down. But it was close to other properties I owned and I knew the location would be okay after previously talking to a couple of salespeople about it.

The owner wanted close to $140,000 and was very keen to sell. We negotiated a price of $135,000 on the phone, on the condition he could arrange with his bank a release from the mortgage. I'm not sure exactly what he owed but it sounded like it was very close to this amount. I wrote up a contract and arranged to see him the following afternoon. In the mean time he had contacted his bank, and all was okay for him to sell at our agreed price. The contract was signed and settlement was to take place in mid January 2015. I sent the contract through to my bank manager to organise the loan documents, as I had done with all the other purchases. He called me back the next day to say they would have to use 80% of the E-Value they had on the property. I said 'okay, is that not what you did on all the other ones?' He said yes all the others were fine but the E-Value on this one is only *$107,000* and the purchase price is $135,000. This meant that normally they would only lend 80% of this amount being $85,600. I mentioned to him that I thought it was worth around $150,000 and would get a valuation done on it. All it meant was that it would have used up some extra equity from my other properties, in other words borrowing equity from them to support this one. The E-Value was way out and this can happen for any number of reasons which is why you can't rely on them for any real accuracy.

I had the registered valuation done and it came out at $160,000 which was about where I thought it would. Now in the banks view, they could lend 80% of this amount being $128,000 which was $7,000 less than I was paying for the property. Now instead of using about $50,000 of equity from my other properties to fund the property ($135,000 - $85,600), it would only use $7,000.

The bank documents were all sorted and sent to my lawyer for me to sign. A week or so later the vendor called me and asked if I could settle the property the week *before* Xmas rather than in mid January. The property was vacant and he didn't want to be paying the mortgage for another month and have no income from tenants. I said I didn't really want to do that as I wouldn't be able to organise for the property to be rented then either, and it would sit vacant for several weeks. He was still keen for me to settle earlier and suggested to me he would take $500 off the price for me to do so. I agreed and it was settled exactly a week before Xmas day 2014.

Katy advertised the property, a new tenant was found and they moved into the property in mid January. My goal was now complete and I had purchased the 20 properties all in one year!

PROPERTY SUMMARY: -

3brm home, garage

Purchase price: $134,500

Rent: $285p.w.

Yield: 11.02% p.a.

Interest rate: 5.55% p.a. fixed for 2 years

Loan term: 20 years

Loan Type: P & I

Cash-flow positive/negative: $2p.w. positive

PROPERTY NUMBER 21!!

HUDSON RD, FLAXMERE

In early December 2014, Katy my property manager was at 'Property Number 14' in Flaxmere talking to the tenant there. It was the property I'd bought around Labour weekend in late October, a 3brm town-house with a garage. The property was attached to the one next door by the garages, and the owner of the one next to mine came outside to talk to Katy. She knew someone had recently bought the property next to her, and therefore asked Katy if she knew if the owner of that one would like to buy *her* one as well. Katy said she would get back to her, or get me to call and I could talk to her. I called the owner and arranged to go out and have a look. She wanted around $115,000 and was keen to sell as she wanted to put an offer on another property in Flaxmere to live in.

I had a look through the property, her one was very similar to the one attached next door that I had recently bought, but needed some interior painting and minor maintenance to be done before it could be tenanted. The garage had been converted into another room now making it 4brms, but there was also a carport and off street parking in another driveway around the corner, as this property was on a corner site. At this stage I didn't really know if I was keen to buy it or not as I already had my 20 properties and wasn't looking for any more. I could have bought it my *original* trust; or I could buy it, renovate it, and sell it on again. If I had renovated the property and sold it on again, there probably wouldn't be a huge margin in it, and so ruled out that option.

We chatted about her situation and what she wanted after I had a look through. There was another property in Flaxmere that she was very keen to buy, but didn't want to make it subject to the sale of her one. The property she had her eye on was a lovely home in a great street and the vendor wanted over $220,000 for it. Any offer I made on her home would need to be subject to her purchasing this property that she was keen on buying. We then talked about the price for her one. I mentioned that I had bought the one next door for $109,000 which was tidier than hers, and I would need to spend some money on her one before it could be tenanted. Also there were no agents' fees to pay, which would save her around $6,000.

We talked for a while and agreed on a price of $105,000; subject to her being able to purchase the other home that she really wanted. At this stage I still wasn't sure if I would put this property in the new trust along with the other recently purchased 20 properties, or in my original trust. We had put down a settlement date of late January 2015 so I had plenty of time to decide, if I did end up buying it.

The next step was for her to make an offer on the other property she wanted to buy, and knowing that she now had an unconditional contract on hers if she wanted it, she was in a much stronger position to be able to negotiate on the other one. After a few days she let me know that she'd managed to get a contract on the other property for less than $220,000. She was very excited and pleased about that, the contract was only 'subject to finance' for five working days which she thought should be approved without any problem.

A few days before Christmas, her finance was all approved and so both properties went unconditional.

The property settled in late January 2015 in the *new trust, and my painter then went through and painted the interior. There were a few other minor repairs we did to the inside of the property, and also some exterior work to the fence and gardens etc. The property was soon completed and was rented for $275p.w.

**In early January 2015 I had decided to put this property into the new trust, but would <u>sell</u> one of the 20 properties I had bought in 2014. The Housing New Zealand 'Property Number 11' that had taken a while to tenant in September was vacant again. The tenants had been on a 90 day trial and my property manager had decided not to keep them on. It had been vacant again for several weeks, and no sign of anyone keen on renting it. I talked to a good friend of mine who also owns a lot of properties in the area and he was keen to buy it. He would build a fence out the front and spend some more money on it to make it a more desirable place to tenant. We agreed on a sale price of $120,000 being $5,000 more than I had paid for it, so I would need to pay tax on that. The property was sold and settled within a few weeks. This left me again with <u>20</u> properties in the new trust.*

Property Number 21 Summary: -

3brm town-house (garage/4th brm), carport

Purchase price: $105,000

Renovation costs: $2,000

Total cost: $107,000

Rent: $275p.w.

Yield: 13.36% p.a.

Interest rate: 5.49% p.a. fixed for 2 years

Loan term: 20 years

Loan Type: P & I

Cash-flow positive/negative: $26p.w. positive

SUMMARY OF THE 20 PROPERTIES

By February 2015, the HNZ property as mentioned above was sold and settled.

I once again had 20 buy and hold properties in the new trust that had been set up a year earlier, and all 20 properties were tenanted.

In Spreadsheet 1 shown on the next page, here is an explanation of each column.

1. the property address.
2. the purchase price of the property; or if renovation work was done, this column shows the total cost.
3. my estimate of market price at the time of purchase. The registered valuations that I got were mostly higher than this amount as mentioned earlier.
4. equity in the property at the time of purchase; this is the market price *minus* the purchase price.
5. rent per week.
6. after rates, insurance, property management and the mortgage payment; this column shows after all those expenses whether the property is cash-flow *positive* or *negative* and by how much, in dollars per week.
7. the amount of principal paid off the loan per month.
   N.B. With a P & I loan, you are paying off some principal (loan balance) every month. At the start of the loan there is usually more interest being paid than principal each month, depending on the term of the loan, and the interest rate. In this case with all the properties being on 20 year loan terms, the principal being paid off each month is approximately 1/3 of the total mortgage payment. For example, if the mortgage payment is $1,000 a month, the principal being paid off is around $330 a month, and the rest ($670) is interest. As time goes by more principal gets paid off and less interest; until near the end of the loan when most of your mortgage payment will be principal, and very little interest is being paid.

SPREADSHEET 1

Address of Property Andorra Holdings Trust	Purchase Price (Including reno if any)	Market Price (approx) At time of purchase	Equity	Rent Per week	Pos/Neg Cash-flow p.w.	Principal paid off loan (month)
Birkenhead Cres Flaxmere	$142,800.00	$185,000.00	$42,200.00	$320.00	$13.00	$330.00
Kingsley Drive Flaxmere	$127,000.00	$155,000.00	$28,000.00	$280.00	$2.50	$300.00
Tenby Tce Flaxmere	$110,000.00	$125,000.00	$15,000.00	$270.00	$21.00	$255.00
Bestall St Napier	$117,000.00	$150,000.00	$33,000.00	$260.00	$3.00	$270.00
Fleming Cres Napier	$111,100.00	$155,000.00	$43,900.00	$275.00	$27.00	$260.00
Geddis Ave Napier	$122,000.00	$150,000.00	$28,000.00	$270.00	$14.00	$270.00
Hotene St Whakatane	$89,500.00	$100,000.00	$10,500.00	$210.00	$5.00	$200.00
Lodge Rd Napier	$113,500.00	$155,000.00	$41,500.00	$290.00	$37.00	$250.00
Geddis Ave Napier	$130,000.00	$160,000.00	$30,000.00	$280.00	$10.00	$285.00
Hotene St Whakatane	$123,000.00	$145,000.00	$22,000.00	$270.00	-$15.00	$270.00
Flaxmere Ave Flaxmere	$125,500.00	$137,000.00	$11,500.00	$250.00	-$2.50	$270.00
Kingsley Drive Flaxmere	$130,000.00	$145,000.00	$15,000.00	$280.00	-$2.50	$280.00
Hudson Road Flaxmere	$109,000.00	$122,000.00	$13,000.00	$265.00	$24.00	$245.00
Dundee Drive Flaxmere	$110,500.00	$150,000.00	$39,500.00	$320.00	$55.00	$270.00
Hood St Hastings	$150,000.00	$165,000.00	$15,000.00	$300.00	-$14.00	$335.00
Caernarvon Drive Flaxmere	$138,500.00	$155,000.00	$16,500.00	$300.00	$10.00	$320.00
Scott Drive Flaxmere	$144,000.00	$160,000.00	$16,000.00	$285.00	-$12.00	$330.00
Shackleton St Napier	$132,000.00	$150,000.00	$18,000.00	$280.00	$5.00	$300.00
Weddell St Flaxmere	$134,500.00	$150,000.00	$15,500.00	$285.00	$2.00	$310.00
Hudson Rd Flaxmere	$105,000.00	$125,000.00	$20,000.00	$275.00	$26.00	$240.00
	$2,464,900.00	**$2,939,000.00**	**$474,100.00**	**$5,585.00**	**$208.50**	**$5,590.00**

The amount of principal that gets paid off monthly varies a lot depending on the interest rate and the term of the loan. At the start of a 30 year loan, a lot less principal is paid each month in your mortgage payment, most of it being interest. As an example, using the same interest rates at the time these loans were taken out if they were all on 30 year mortgages, rather than $330 being paid off each month at the start of the loan, only about $150 per month would have been paid off.
A great website to have a look at is http://bretwhissel.net/amortization/. You can put in various loan amounts, interest rates and loan terms to see what sort of difference all these variables make. It's very interesting to see how much of a factor these all make, especially to see how much interest you are paying over the term of a loan.

At the bottom of each column is the *total* amounts added together.

With this 1st Spreadsheet you will see the equity total is $474,100. This is the approx dollar amount that was made over all 20 properties in equity gained by purchasing *below* market price. This works out to be an average of around $23,700 *per* property over the 20 properties. You will also see the cash-flow *total* per week is $208.50 *positive*; most properties worked out positive each week and a few slightly negative. This figure is after the mortgage payment, rates, insurance and property management has been taken out of the rent received, but it doesn't allow for any maintenance. The final column shows that a total of $5,590 is being paid off the total loan balance ($2,464,900) each month. As mentioned previously, this amount increases slightly each month, around $1 per month *per* loan. With 20 loans; for each month that goes by, approx $20 (20 x $1) *more* than the previous month gets paid off the principal. So the following month approx $5,610 would be paid off the total principal amount owing, then $5,630, $5,650, $5,670 and so on.

If you now have a look at Spreadsheet 2, you will see that the principal being paid off has *increased* to $5,900 a month. The cash-flow has also increased to $857 per week. This is due partly to rent increases but mostly due to the monthly mortgage payments being less now with the *lower* interest rates. When taking out the 20 loans, the interest rates varied from 5.49%p.a. up to 5.99%p.a.

Spreadsheet 2

Address of Property Andorra Holdings Trust	Mortgage Owing (LoanBalance)	Market Price (approx) As at July 2016	Equity	Rent Per week	Pos/Neg Cash-flow p.w.	Principal paid off loan (month)
Birkenhead Cres Flaxmere	$132,272.00	$215,000.00	$82,728.00	$320.00	$42.00	$350.00
Kingsley Drive Flaxmere	$117,636.00	$180,000.00	$62,364.00	$285.00	$35.00	$270.00
Tenby Tce Flaxmere	$109,230.00	$162,500.00	$53,270.00	$280.00	$47.00	$320.00
Bestall St Napier	$106,335.00	$185,000.00	$78,665.00	$280.00	$49.00	$315.00
Fleming Cres Napier	$103,395.00	$190,000.00	$86,605.00	$275.00	$52.00	$270.00
Geddis Ave Napier	$112,226.00	$180,000.00	$67,774.00	$310.00	$57.00	$290.00
Hotene St Whakatane	$84,512.00	$115,000.00	$30,488.00	$225.00	$31.00	$220.00
Lodge Rd Napier	$107,197.00	$190,000.00	$82,803.00	$290.00	$50.00	$270.00
Geddis Ave Napier	$122,474.00	$190,000.00	$67,526.00	$280.00	$37.00	$300.00
Hotene St Whakatane	$116,828.00	$157,500.00	$40,672.00	$270.00	$26.00	$280.00
Flaxmere Ave	$119,533.00	$180,000.00	$60,467.00	$290.00	$43.00	$280.00
Kingsley Drive Flaxmere	$124,098.00	$180,000.00	$55,902.00	$290.00	$37.00	$290.00
Hudson Road Flaxmere	$103,919.00	$160,000.00	$56,081.00	$275.00	$53.00	$280.00
Dundee Drive Flaxmere	$114,406.00	$185,000.00	$70,594.00	$320.00	$79.00	$260.00
Hood St Hastings	$142,767.00	$195,000.00	$52,233.00	$300.00	$18.00	$345.00
Caernarvon Drive Flaxmere	$131,900.00	$185,000.00	$53,100.00	$300.00	$34.00	$340.00
Scott Drive Flaxmere	$137,138.00	$185,000.00	$47,862.00	$285.00	$13.00	$330.00
Shackleton St Napier	$124,137.00	$195,000.00	$70,863.00	$285.00	$33.00	$320.00
Weddell St Flaxmere	$129,922.00	$180,000.00	$50,078.00	$315.00	$54.00	$310.00
Hudson Rd Flaxmere	$100,517.00	$162,500.00	$61,983.00	$290.00	$67.00	$260.00
	$2,340,442.00	**$3,572,500.00**	**$1,232,058.00**	**$5,765.00**	**$857.00**	**$5,900.00**

The interest rate I have been fixing the loans as they've been coming off these fixed rates is 4.15%p.a. fixed for two years. As at the time of writing this, most loans are still fixed for between another one month and another six months before they come off the higher rates. I have calculated the cash-flow for each property based on 4.15%p.a. however if the interest rate is slightly higher or lower than this when I do fix them in the next few months, this weekly cash-flow amount will change slightly.

If you now look at the total mortgage amount owing in column 2 of Spreadsheet 2, this has reduced by over $120,000 since the loans started (from column 2 of Spreadsheet 1). This is due to the principal amounts of now almost $6,000 being paid off *each* month over the 20 loans.

It was in reality approximately $20,000 better than this because of two separate things. The first was with the Dundee Dr property which is Property Number 15. The total after reno cost for this property was $110,500 and you may remember the amount I borrowed was $120,000. This meant that I borrowed $9,500 *more* than my total costs. If you look at this property in the two spreadsheets, you will see the amount owing now on the mortgage ($114,000) is still more than the original total cost after reno ($110,500).

The other anomaly was that when I sold the Arbroath Ave property (Number 11), I swapped the loan on that one for the Tenby Tce (Property Number 3) loan. I did this because there was going to be high break fees on the Arbroath Ave loan at the time of selling it, as the mortgage had only been recently fixed on its two year term. Also with all of these loans taken out, the bank was paying me a cash contribution of $1,000 upon each settlement; so this would have also had to be paid back if paying off this loan in full after such a short time. My bank manager suggested we instead pay off the Tenby Tce loan as he could arrange paying it off in full with no break fees and not paying back the cash contribution. The higher Arbroath Ave loan therefore was transferred to the lower Tenby Tce loan. This meant that I received the difference back between the two loans of about $9,000 upon settlement, plus the extra $5,000 more that the property was sold for.

So if you look at the Tenby Tce property in both spreadsheets, the loan in Spreadsheet 2 is approx $109,000 (originally $110,000) whereas it would have been down to around $100,000 had the *original* loan continued. In summary what this means is that I received back nearly $20,000 with these two things happening. This amount was added to the original loans of

Spreadsheet 1 and these now show up in Spreadsheet 2. In other words about *$140,000* has been paid off the principal in total on the 20 loans, but it shows that only around *$120,000* has been paid off as the other $20,000 was received back into my account. So, if you think about the original plan of buying all the properties and using no equity; it worked out even better than this as I was 20,000 better off than when I started. No money turned into buying 20 self-sustaining properties that are gaining equity every month until they are all paid off in 20 years time, plus $20,000 back as a result of buying them!

If you look at the 3rd column in Spreadsheet 2, the total value of the properties is now over $3,500,000. That's my estimate of the current values of all 20 properties combined at the time of writing this. The total market value of the 20 properties therefore has increased by over $600,000 in 2 ½ years. To me, this is the least important column, as next year or the year after they could lose $600,000 in value or even more. The most important thing to remember is that whatever prices may or may not do in the future, the loans are all slowly getting paid down. At this stage around $5,900 a month gets paid off the total amount owing on the mortgages and this amount increases slightly every month as previously mentioned.

The 4th column in each spreadsheet shows the total equity in the 20 properties combined. In Spreadsheet 1, the total equity was $474,100. In Spreadsheet 2, this has now grown to around $1,232,000 or an increase of more than $750,000 in 2 ½ years. Most of this is due to the increase in market prices since 2014, and the balance of it is in equity gained since taking out the loans (approx $120,000 as mentioned earlier).

As time goes by, each loan balance will slowly reduce each month no matter what the market prices may do. Market prices may rise, fall, or stay the same but the loan balance will *always* reduce every month with the principal being paid off. So in another 17 ½ years time when all the loans are paid off in full, I don't really care what each property is worth, or what its market value is. They may be worth what I paid for them in 2014 or maybe even less, or they could have doubled or quadrupled in value or more – I don't mind. What I *do* care about is the cash-flow and the weekly rent from each property.

In the 5th column of Spreadsheet 2, you will see the total rents are now $5,765 per week. I allow around 25% of this amount for rates, insurance and property management. When you ask to borrow money from a bank for any rental property, they also use around 75% of the total rent received, and base their numbers on this. You will of course have some maintenance that needs doing from time to time on each property; this can vary somewhat, but so far as mentioned earlier, it has worked out to be around $50 a *month* for each property ($1,000 in total over 20 properties), over the last 2 ½ years.

So let's say the rents when all the loans are paid off are still consistent with the current rents of $5,765 a week, this works out to be just under $25,000 a month. If you then allow 25% of this for rates, insurance and property management, you end up with approximately $18,750 a month in cash-flow. And remember all this was created by using one *simple idea* and a goal, the idea to buy 10 properties well, which then went on to become 20 properties. The goal was to finance these properties at 100% of purchase price, therefore not use any of my existing cash or equity, and for all the loans to be paid off in 20 years. Now 2 ½ years later from having this initial idea and goal, it has worked out even better than I had hoped for or planned. The experiment that started out from one simple idea has turned into a huge success; and I'm happy to have been able to share it with you and how it was all done, in this book. ☺

YOU CAN'T DO THAT *NOW!!!*

Over the last 15 years or more I've chatted to several thousand property investors throughout New Zealand. This has been either through e-mail, Facebook, property investment forums, seminars I've spoken at or attended, or in person. One thing that comes up a lot is people saying 'you can't do that now' or 'you wouldn't be able to do that now'. I've also heard it from lawyers, accountants, bank managers, real estate salespeople, financial planners and tradespeople etc, but the biggest concern is when I hear it from other property investors. They will say things like 'it was okay when you did it, times were different then, but it's not possible to do that today', or 'you got in at the right time, it's not possible to do what you did now'. During 2000 and 2001 when I started buying and investing in property seriously, it was a *decision* I made to go out and buy a lot of property. A decision that resulted as mentioned in one of the earlier articles at the start of this book. A lot of people even immediately after buying those 60 properties within two years said 'you couldn't do that now'. I didn't give it a lot of thought then, but it has come up more and more over the last 15 years, people saying the same thing. I guess part of the experiment in 2014 that I wrote about in Part 3 of this book was to show others that it *could* be done. I wrote up a new thread on PropertyTalk.com at the end of 2013 of what I was intending to do. Here is the link to it if you would like to read through all the pages of posts, updates etc. https://www.propertytalk.com/forum/showthread.php?34555-Property-Investment-Different-Strategy

Out of the 40,000 or so members on Property Talk, not one of the investors said 'what a great idea, I'm going to set a goal, and see if I can do the same thing as well'. While I have many friends I know on the site, and most are very encouraging and have different goals, strategies and plans with their investing, there are a lot of other experienced investors on the forum which could have said 'I'm going to give this a go too'. If you do get a chance to have a look and read through the posts (over 500) and just think of the mindset of the people writing the posts. I think I mentioned in some of my posts that it's not really a wise strategy for someone just starting out with their investing because of the risks involved if they don't have a good solid foundation to start with. But there are many experienced investors on there that already have a reasonably solid foundation and could have done the same or a similar thing as to what I did. Anyway, you can have a look for yourself if you are interested in reading some of the comments.

The point is after the 2014 year when all the 20 properties had been purchased and were ticking along well, I got a lot of comments in 2015 telling me again that it *couldn't be done now*! 'Prices have gone up and you just can't get those same deals now' people would say. I said to them 'but interest rates are lower now too, so your overall cash-flow still works out about the same'. It never changed peoples' thoughts on it though as they would just offer another excuse. It all comes down to a person's mindset, beliefs, attitude and behaviours. If they don't believe they can do it, then using an excuse like 'you can't do that *now*' allows them to go back into their comfort zone.

What Stops You?

As mentioned in the introduction, we now have the new 40% deposit rule for investors which has only just come into effect. This will no doubt stop a lot of investors too, giving them another excuse as to why it was easier before, but you can't do that *now*. If you are just starting out, will you let it stop you? Or will you carry on and work out a way around it that helps you move forward and reach your goals?

Over the years, many investors have sold up what they own because of things like this. A few years ago we had the government change the depreciation rule so that you could no longer claim depreciation on investment properties you owned. Lots of investors sold because of this. More recently we have had the meth (P) issue and there is a lot of uncertainty about it, I also know of investors that have sold because of this. I know of other investors that have sold everything for fear of the possible new WOF rules that may come in for rental properties. All sorts of possibilities and happenings that some investors will get frightened about the unknown, forget about all their goals and their plan, and decide to sell up. Now we have the new LVR rule, and nobody knows if it's here to stay or is just a temporary thing. The question is – will it stop you from beginning if you're a new investor, or will it make you want to sell everything if you've already been investing for some time? Where is the point that you would say 'enough is enough' and want to stop? Personally I've found that when any new laws or changes come into effect, it has usually made things easier for me as an investor, not harder as many assume it will.

Today we have interest rates at an all time low and if I was starting again today, armed with the knowledge I have today as well, I would think now is as good a time as any that I've seen in the past, to make a start.

What ideas or goals do you have that you've wanted to do for a long time, but as yet have not taken any action? What's preventing you from taking that first step; is it the fear of the unknown, or the fear of *possibly* failing? One of my favourite quotes is one that I read over 30 years ago which says - "It's better to attempt something great and fail, than to attempt to do nothing and succeed". If I can fail School C English and later on write a best selling property book in NZ, what could *you* do?

I would now encourage you to go back and read the introduction of this book again (yes I know it is very long ☺).

If you have read the entire book, you will be reading it now from a *new* perspective, or a new you. You will read it and understand it on a new and deeper level. There are many tapes and CDs I've listened to and books I've read over the last 30 years. And every time I listen to a CD again, or read a book that I've already read before, there's always something new I get from it. Something I never heard or saw before, or maybe never really understood. Often it's like 'how did I miss that before?' or, 'is this the same CD I've already listened to 20 times before, I'm sure that was not in there before!'

You are welcome to email me anytime on orion8@xtra.co.nz and remember to join the free "Property Investors Chat Group NZ"on Facebook if you are not already a member, or Katrina's "Women in Property Investing NZ". If you aren't able to find them, look me up on Facebook and send me a message so I can send you a link to join.

I wish you every success in whatever you choose to do and the goals and dreams you may have.

Thank you and safe investing ☺

RECOMMENDED READING

Allen, James *As A Man Thinketh*

Allen, Robert *Nothing Down*

Allen, Robert *Multiple Streams of Income*

Allen, Robert *The One Minute Millionaire*

Bettger, Frank *How I Raised Myself From Failure to Success in Selling*

Burley, John *Australia's Money Secrets of the Rich*

Carnegie, Dale *How to Win friends and Influence People*

Clason, George S *The Richest Man in Babylon*

Chopra, Deepak *Creating Affluence*

Coelho, Paulo *The Alchemist*

Covey, Stephen R *The 7 Habits of Highly Effective People*

Covey, Stephen R *A Roger Merrill and Rebecca R Merrill First Things First*

DeGreen, Keith *What Millionaires Know About Money*

Eklund, Fredrik *The Sell*

Fisher, Mark *The Golfer and the Millionaire*

Fowler, Graeme *NZ Real Estate Investors' Secrets*

Fuller, Buckminster R *Critical Path*

Goodwin, Charles *The Secrets of Wealth Creation Revealed*

Hamilton, Roger *Your Life Your Legacy*

Hamilton, Roger *Wink and Grow Rich (Wink)*

Hicks, Esther & Jerry *Ask and it is Given*

Hicks, Esther & Jerry *Getting into the Vortex*

Hicks, Esther & Jerry *Money and the Law of Attraction*

Hicks, Esther & Jerry *Sara – Book 1, 2 & 3*

Hicks, Esther & Jerry *The Amazing Power of Deliberate Intent*

Hicks, Esther & Jerry *The Astonishing Power of Your Emotions*

Hicks, Esther & Jerry *The Law of Attraction*

Hill, Napolean *Think and Grow Rich*

Jeffers, Susan *Feel the Fear and Do It Anyway*

Jones, Bob *Jones on Property*

Jones, Bob *My Property Journey*

Kiyosaki, Robert T *Cashflow Quadrant*

Kiyosaki, Robert T *If You Want to Be Rich & Happy, Don't Go to School*

Kiyosaki, Robert T *Rich Dad, Poor Dad*

Lowndes, Leil *How to Talk to Anyone*

MacGregor, Sandy *Piece of Mind*

Mulford, Prentice *Thoughts are Things*

Proctor, Bob *You were Born Rich*

Robbins, Anthony *Awaken the Giant Within You*

Robbins, Anthony *Unlimited Power*

Schucman, Helen *A Course In Miracles*

Schwartz, David *The Magic of Thinking Big*

Schwartz, David *The Magic of Thinking Success*

Sharma, Robin *The Monk who sold his Ferrari*

Sher, Brian *What Rich People Know & Desperately Want to Keep a Secret*

Singer, Blair *Sales Dogs*

Spann, Peter *Wealth Magic*

Stanley, Thomas J *The Millionaire Next Door*

Sugars, Bradley J *Billionaire in Training*

Walsch, Neal Donald *Conversations With God – Books 1, 2 & 3*

Wattles, Wallace D *The Science of Getting Rich*

Whitecloud, William *The Magician's Way*

Whitney, Russ *Building Wealth*